ch
497

D0687215

DATE DUE

JE 18 '98			

Six Timeless Marketing Blunders

Six Timeless Marketing Blunders

by
William L. Shanklin

Lexington Books

D.C. Heath and Company / Lexington, Massachusetts / Toronto

Library of Congress Cataloging-in-Publication Data

Shanklin, William L.
Six timeless marketing blunders / by William Shanklin.
p.   cm.

Includes index.
ISBN 0-669-19499-9 (alk. paper)
1. Marketing—Management. I. Title.
HF5415.13.S46   1989
658.8—dc19   88-28116
                                              CIP

Published simultaneously in Canada
Printed in the United States of America
International Standard Book Number: 0-669-19499-9
Library of Congress Catalog Card Number: 88-28116

The paper used in this publication meets the minimum requirements
of American National Standard for Information Sciences—Permanence
of Paper for Printed Library Materials, ANSI Z39.48-1984.

∞™

89 90 91 92 8 7 6 5 4 3 2 1

*This book is dedicated to the
individual and corporate entrepreneurs
(past and present)
who, at great personal risk and sacrifice,
make life better for all of us.
To these usually obscure and frequently
unlikely engines of progress who dare to
fail—and more often than not do—
we owe the economic vigor, jobs, and
standard of living flowing from new
businesses, technologies, products,
and services.*

Contents

For of all sad words of tongue and pen
The saddest are these: "It might have been."
                    —John Greenleaf Whittier

Preface

The most prevalent and fatal commercial mistakes that entrepreneurs and companies make are marketing or market-related. One of the leading venture capitalists, who has looked at thousands of business plans and helped to launch many firms, says there are two reasons why companies fail. The first is lack of sales, and the second is lack of everything else. A startup business or new product or service usually fails because the firm does not satisfy enough customers, or does not do it better than the competition.

Since time immemorial, the same marketing blunders have been committed over and over again, from generation to generation. Whenever I see an entrepreneur or company struggling with a business, product, or service, I am reminded of what former New York Yankee catcher Yogi Berra once said: "It was déjà vu all over again."

The six marketing blunders around which I have structured this book are the ones I believe are the most harmful and also the most recurring. These timeless blunders will remain timeless; this book could be rewritten a hundred years from now, changing only the examples, and be current.

Largely because of these six classic marketing mistakes, history will repeat itself and far more startup businesses and new products and services will fail than succeed. The odds of being included among the success stories can be improved by learning to recognize the thinking that leads to the blunders and also by taking steps to minimize the risks of committing them. I hope this book will assist fledgling entrepreneurs, small business people, and corporate developers/marketers of products and services to do that, and thus to increase their chances of writing their own versions of commercial stories with happy outcomes.

Introduction

What prompted me to write a book called *Six Timeless Marketing Blunders*? Here is a brief explanation of how the idea evolved.

I have had the opportunity and privilege to work with and observe many people seeking to develop and market a diversity of products and services. They ranged from aspiring entrepreneurs and inventors to executives in giant corporations. Regardless of whether the person was trying to run a business from home—perhaps an inventor with a laboratory in the garage or basement—or the person was in a high-technology company with elaborate research facilities and complex goods and services to offer, the same kinds of questions about the entrepreneurial process kept recurring and intriguing me.

A Serendipity Effect?

The question I became most intrigued by was whether successful entrepreneurship is the result more of being in the right place at the right time or of skill and effort. How important a role does luck play in determining whether a person succeeds in starting and growing a business or commercializing a new product or service? Put differently, in most entrepreneurial success stories, is there a serendipity effect at work? We all know of rags-to-riches journeys in which the man or woman involved appears to have stumbled into fame and fortune, or in which some product that becomes a household name is the result of happenstance.

Many years ago, American circuses would take laughing gas on tour with them for entertainment purposes. Customers would inhale the fumes and literally have a hilarious time. One day a customer who had partaken passed out, fell off a platform, and broke his leg. A physician in the crowd came forward to put the leg into a splint and saw that the injured man was literally laughing despite his ordeal. From this chance occurrence, the doctor realized that laughing gas can be used as an anesthetic. Or take another example. An early-1900s London restaurant goofed by serving Nellie Melba, a virtuoso soprano of the times, overcooked dry toast. When the dieting opera star found it to her liking, the maître d' alertly christened it in her honor, thereby creating fortune from a mistake.

Even in large companies, serendipity or luck sometimes enters the picture in the discovery of what prove to be highly profitable offerings. Post-it Note Pads, Valium, and Nutrasweet were to some extent all lucky finds.

I have concluded that serendipity does usually come into play in successful entrepreneurial endeavors, but that it takes an innovative and gutsy person to exploit the opportunity. Legendary oil wildcatter H.L. Hunt would not have struck it rich drilling for oil if he had not been drilling. And Walt Disney was filming before he became a great filmmaker.

An Entrepreneurial Personality?

In my judgment, almost all successful entrepreneurs and marketers of new products and services share two key qualities—perseverance or drive, and resilience in the face of rejection and defeat. Some of the richest self-made people today did not finish high school; others completed college, and a few earned advanced degrees. So education is not the common thread—it is perseverance and resilience. Many entrepreneurial ventures are prompted by misfortune, often when someone is laid off from a job or fired. *Success* magazine gives annual awards to individuals, mostly entrepreneurs, who have made great comebacks—people who have fought their way back from crushing adversity to succeed mightily. These stories are truly remarkable and eloquently illustrate what I am referring to here about tenacity and resilience.

Nobby Lewandowski, a certified public accountant, exemplifies these traits. He went through college on a baseball scholarship and graduated with a self-described average academic record, although he later earned an MBA. After college he had a short-lived career in professional baseball in the minor leagues and with the Pittsburgh Pirates long enough for a cup of coffee. One of his cherished memories is of sitting on the bench next to Roberto Clemente. His baseball career over, Lewandowski was hired by a leading CPA firm. After several years, he was let go, but not because of his work. He was let go because he stutters. Lewandowski's boss said something to the effect, "As you advance in the business world and work with a CPA firm, you meet with hurried executives. Communication skills are important. And . . ." Lewandowski's stammering was thought to interfere with high-level client relations.

Today, he is prosperous, the owner of his own CPA firm in Medina, Ohio, and a marvelous inspiration to others by example and through motivational speaking with his speech impediment intact.

The main reason for his own success, Lewandowski says, is that he hires people to work for him who are a lot smarter than he is. "But," he observes wryly, "I sign their paychecks." Like most other successful entrepreneurs, he perseveres and takes both the good and the bad in stride. There is tomorrow and a new horizon and challenges to look forward to. Not content with yesterday, one of Lewandowski's goals is to meet one new person every day.

Entrepreneurial sorts do not spend their lives majoring in minors. They know there is enough adversity without becoming immobilized by concentrating on things they cannot control. They play the cards dealt them by life. Nobby Lewandowski did not give up when his employment was terminated with the large CPA firm; the incident spurred him on. He did not get even—he got successful and is helping others do the same. These kinds of stories are commonplace among entrepreneurs—ghetto men and women founding businesses from impossible surroundings, widows with young mouths to feed starting businesses after the deaths of their husbands, and eighth-grade dropouts overcoming their education handicap to launch and build companies.

People with entrepreneurial qualities may fail and fail again, but they come back. Like the mythical phoenix, they rise from the ashes of a failed business or product to try again and again. Like a champion boxer knocked to the canvas, they try to get up. If and when an entrepreneur finally does make it big, some observers on the sideline invariably attribute it solely to luck.

The real estate developer, sportsman, and philanthropist, John W. Galbreath, achieved immense fame and fortune from beginnings as a poor Ohio farm boy. When he died recently at 90, condolences to the Galbreath family came from people from all walks of life—from a waitress at his business club to Queen Elizabeth II of England. In his eulogy to John Galbreath, Norman Vincent Peale told of the time a reporter asked Galbreath for the secret of success in business. Galbreath's brief but expressive answer: "Intense desire. You have to want to with all your heart. And then, secondly, love people and be good to them. And thirdly, you've got to think and work, and work and think. And finally, leave the world a better place than you found it."

One entrepreneur and small-business owner told me that there are many days when he would like to walk out and leave the hassle behind. But he never does. The executive heading the vast operations of a major manufacturer and marketer said that several years ago, while driving to work, he decided to resign because his company was making shoddy products. He changed his mind and resolved to turn the quality situation around instead—which he did.

I heard one of the wealthiest men in the United States (who began with nothing) say confidently but not boastfully that if he does not succeed today on a project or venture, he will tomorrow or the day after that. Nobby Lewandowski, the CPA, told me that all his clients who are self-made millionaires are extremely early risers, anxious to compete with the dawning of another day. Unlike the person who plays the lottery hoping to get rich fast, entrepreneurial types—in small businesses or large companies—put great faith in their ability to control their fate. Their credo seems to be that luck is infatuated with effort. Like William Jennings Bryan, they feel that "destiny is a matter of choice."

Are Entrepreneurs and Entrepreneurial Executives Born or Made?

My observations about the psychological makeup—the incredible perseverance and resilience—that successful entrepreneurs tend to have in common led me to ponder another question: Can entrepreneurship be taught, or is it innate? You surely cannot teach someone to have fortitude. The matter of teaching entrepreneurship happens to be a topic being debated today. My own judgment is that you cannot teach a person to be an entrepreneur or an entrepreneurial executive if the individual does not already have the requisite bulldog tenacity and resilience—the personality to cope with the inevitable setbacks and uncertainties. However, people possessing these entrepreneurial qualities may also prove to be total failures at starting businesses or commercializing new products and services—if they do not know how.

You can indeed teach people with entrepreneurial personalities, for the lack of a better term, the elements of entrepreneurship—how to write a business plan, where to seek financing, how to interface R&D and marketing, how to organize a new-product management team, and how to bid for small-business set-asides by the federal government. What you cannot do is to look into someone's heart and see if he or she has what it takes. A written test to measure entrepreneurial tendencies may indicate a person's general suitability, but it will not reveal how the person will react the first time the payroll is due and there is no cash. Or, in a large company, what the individual in R&D or marketing will do when the boss wants to terminate a promising project because of cost overruns.

The subject of teaching and learning entrepreneurship brings me to the purpose of this book. The risks of starting businesses and commercializing products and services in going concerns are considerable. Nothing can reduce the risks to zero. But the risks can be tempered—and I hope that is how this book can contribute. Countless people with the resolve and motivation to start businesses from scratch or to bring products and services to market in existing companies have been or will be thwarted by one or more of the six blunders considered in this book. One former entrepreneur commented that he had fallen prey to all six. If this book can help steer a few of these individuals away from a disaster course and toward the road to success, I will consider it to have been of value. As I said in my dedication, new businesses, technologies, products, and services are what produce economic vigor, jobs, and a better standard of living for all of us.

1
Life on the Razor's Edge

If people learn from their mistakes, many are getting a fantastic education.

It took former J.C. Penney employee Sam Walton, law-school dropout Leslie Wexner, and one-time IBM salesman H. Ross Perot less than thirty years to found and grow companies that propelled them to the top of the *Forbes* magazine list of wealthiest Americans. In stark contrast, over 50 percent of the companies on *Fortune* magazine's original 1955 list of the largest U.S. industrial firms were no longer on it thirty years later. Once prominent companies like Beaunit Mills, Hercules Powder, Liebman Breweries, and Youngstown Sheet and Tube were replaced by upstarts such as Amdahl, Inspiration Resources, LaFarge, and Liquid Air.

Between 1970 and 1981, 29 percent of the *Fortune* 500 firms vanished as companies. Between 1980 and 1986, the *Fortune* 500 companies cut 2.8 million jobs. Between 1981 and 1985, companies employing more than five hundred people created 27 percent of the new jobs in the United States but also accounted for 42 percent of the job losses, for a net loss of 15 percent. In the same short time, companies employing fewer than twenty people were responsible for 33 percent of new jobs and 14 percent of job losses, for a net gain of 19 percent. Some of the largest companies, however, have fared much better than others. Service companies and defense and technology firms dominate the list of large companies that have created jobs in recent years. While such companies as Chrysler, MCI Communications, Northrop, and Sears, Roebuck have been providing new employment, others like Caterpillar, Gulf +

Western, Union Carbide, and Westinghouse Electric have been active job cutters.

"Shirtsleeves to Shirtsleeves in Three Generations"

Self-employment has exploded in the United States, with women starting businesses at two to three times the rate of men. During the 1980s, an average of 600,000 businesses were incorporated each year, plus perhaps 500,000 new unincorporated businesses that chose to operate initially as sole proprietorships or partnerships. By comparison, the average number of new businesses incorporated annually in the 1970s and 1960s was 365,000 and 205,000, respectively.

This flurry of economic change and restructuring is the renewal process at work, which brilliant economist Joseph Schumpeter has called "creative destruction." New jobs come from small and flourishing companies, old and mainline industries are reduced in importance by growing industries—many based on revolutionary technologies—and some companies and industries vanish entirely.

In his book *Capitalism, Socialism, and Democracy*, Schumpeter wrote that capitalism is a form or method of economic change that neither can be nor is stationary. There is a constant changing of the guard for the good of society as a whole. Change, Schumpeter said, is a greater barrier to economic monopoly than any law could be, and progress as a society depends on it. Change means that the most adept economic competitors will survive, the ones proving themselves in the marketplace by satisfying societal needs, while the ones that do not will perish. That is why the *Fortune* 500 list continually has companies coming and leaving. That is why entrepreneurs have the opportunity to build companies by outcompeting established corporations that would otherwise be insulated from marketplace pressures. That is why free market economies outperform state-directed economies. A free marketplace is a continual form of revolution, bringing more change for societal good than any government could ever hope to achieve through central planning. Compared to a free marketplace, Lenin himself would pale as a revolutionary force. Government's proper role in capitalism is to provide a safety net for the people who lose their jobs and whose skills are obsolete while, at the same time, not interfering with or impeding the inexorable entrepreneurial renewal process—the innovation, the new technologies, products, services, and industries—that leads to a higher and higher standard of living.

Andrew Carnegie, observing that it is hard for the heirs of a family fortune to perpetuate the wealth, remarked, "Shirtsleeves to shirtsleeves in three generations." Unlike Europe, where family wealth often lasts several centuries, in the United States it tends to dissipate quickly. For example, only a very few families on the *Forbes* magazine list of wealthiest Americans can trace their fortunes back to before the Civil War.

Silk to Denim or Denim to Silk in One Generation

The U.S. economy is so changeable today, with revolutionary technologies and global competition, that Andrew Carnegie's three generations are too long. Success or failure can be quick in coming and quick in going. Ambitious people and upstart companies can go from denim to silk in one generation—or, for the establishment resting on their laurels or making wrong decisions, from silk to cotton or even denim.

Anyone operating in today's fast-paced world economy is in an inherently risky line of work—whether that anyone be a freelance entrepreneur seeking personal enhancement or an upper-level executive with a giant corporation trying to preserve and augment stockholder wealth. Consider the environment in which new and old products, services, and ventures must compete: discerning consumers, intense global competition, rapid technological progress, immense social, economic, and political change, and corporate raiders. It is life on the razor's edge. Speaking of the ever-present threat of a takeover, the chairman of a major company compared his role to that of a Daniel Boone–type pioneer threatened by Indians—to those days of yesteryear when you plowed your fields with an eye peeled for hostiles and a gun slung over your shoulder.

Freedom to Succeed, Freedom to Fail

In an entrepreneurial economy, freedom brings with it upside opportunity and downside risk. Those are the rules rightly imposed by an impartial market. One can make a fortune or go bankrupt. And the failure rate for new business ventures in free societies is high, although estimates vary as to just how high. A conservative estimate is that a third of the new businesses in the United States do not last six years. Likewise, the failure rate for new products and services commercialized by going companies, rather than start-up businesses, is thought to average 70 to 80 percent or higher. For some of the companies, say a premier marketer like H.J. Heinz, the failure rate will be much lower than it will be for smaller companies with less experience in and resources for commercializing products and services.

The process of creative destruction affords great opportunity to those who seize upon it, and it threatens those who do not adapt. For instance, what will a population boom of older citizens mean to companies now prospering? Some companies will be skewered by it, while others will profit. It is an excellent bet that firms yet to be founded will become household names as they devise strategies for catering to the needs and wants of baby boomers grown old. What will be the fate of traditional newspapers and publishers in a dichotomous society with a large segment of aged people who may read less than they once did, and a high-tech-reared segment of younger people who prefer fast-paced electronic media and videotapes to the printed page?

Constants Amid Change

Many business ventures and products and services that fail do so for marketing-related reasons. There are no sure-fire recipes or formulas for success when one group of individuals—entrepreneurs or executives in a company—are trying to divine what another group of people—customers or potential customers—might think enough of to buy and continue to buy. Additionally, marketing strategy encompasses so many activities having to do with satisfying customers—product development and quality, distribution, advertising and personal selling, and pricing, to name a few—that it leaves plenty of room for making mistakes. There are so many places things can go wrong.

Even so, certain classes or genres of strategic, as opposed to tactical, marketing mistakes are prevalent. A very few erroneous ideas and practices have time and again prevented entrepreneurs and managers from achieving their objectives. I have selected for consideration the six that I see as the most troublesome.

For anyone about to start a business or market a product or service, how can he or she recognize that one of the errors is about to be made? What can be done to mitigate the risks of failure? I asked these questions of Stanley C. Gault, chairman of the board and chief executive officer of Rubbermaid, who was previously a top executive with General Electric. He is also past chairman of the National Association of Manufacturers. In my judgment, Gault is one of the most skilled CEOs active today, an executive with the competence of Lee Iacocca but without the bluster. In 1987, he was named American Manager of the Year by the National Management Association and was presented his award by President Reagan. In his career, he has been involved in bringing countless products to market. Rubbermaid has been honored for several years by *Fortune* magazine as being one of America's most admired corporations.

Question: Why do you think that the failure rate is so high for startup businesses and for products and services that going concerns try to commercialize?

Gault: The principal reason for failure is the absence of a comprehensive and realistic business plan. Without such a road map, it is easy to misjudge the size of the market, underestimate the strength and reaction from competition, difficulty involved to gain new distribution, necessary financial resources including a conservative cash flow projection, and overlook the imperativeness to include a viable contingency action plan.

Question: From your experiences at General Electric and Rubbermaid, what have you found is the best way(s) to take some of the risks out of commercializing new products and services?

Answer: Realistically evaluating the potential total market, projected market share, thoroughly evaluating the marketing research information to determine customer acceptance of the product and projected pricing levels and developing a complete and effective advertising and merchandising program. It is too easy to have emotion and personal feelings take precedence over the factors to consider for any new product or service introduction.

Question: If you were counseling an aspiring entrepreneur (with an idea for a product, service, or new venture), what would be the single most important piece of advice you would give?

Answer: The need to develop a comprehensive and realistic business plan which includes conservative financial projections, anticipates competitive reactions, and a possible economic downturn.

Questions to Ask Yourself

1. Do you have a comprehensive written business plan for the product you want to market or the company you want to start?

2. If so, are your objectives, strategies, and expectations conservative and realistically supported by the facts at hand and market research? Are there enough facts at hand?

3. Do you have a contingency plan?

2
Blunder #1:
Building Better Mousetraps

If a man can write a better book, preach a better sermon, or make
a better mousetrap than his neighbor, though he builds his house in
the woods, the world will make a beaten path to his door.
                                —Ralph Waldo Emerson, 1869 lecture

As a poet and essayist, Emerson had few peers. But his philosophy about writing books, preaching sermons, and building
mousetraps has been the downfall of many entrepreneurial efforts.

Emerson would have been a lousy marketing strategist. Shake-
speare does not sell well outside academia, while sensationalized
and lurid books become best-sellers. Which literature is better?
Neighborhood clergy worry about attendance and money, while
television evangelists garner publicity and sometimes wealth, occasionally in the face of scandal. Which approach to ministering
is better? Many technologically elegant products fail in the marketplace, while simpler ones sell. Is high technology better than low
technology?

When I appeared on a television phone-in show dealing with
how to start a business, a caller asked me why his efforts to sell
his product had failed. He went on to say that his product is
"superior" to those already on the market, but that he could find
no one that thought enough of it to distribute it for him. I tried
to explain in thirty seconds that what constitutes a superior product is in the eye of the beholder—and that the world rarely beats
a path to anybody's door. In addition, what if there are no mice
in the area to create demand for his better mousetrap?

The caller's way of thinking has caused problems for marketers
—from independent entrepreneurs to premier companies—ever since

barter was the system of exchange. The pertinent issue in evaluating commercial opportunity is, Who says the product or service is better—the seller or the potential buyers?

Emerson's philosophy lives on in the hearts and minds of countless entrepreneurs and businesses today, from one-office proprietorships to the executive suites of giant companies. Building-better-mousetrap thinking is the number-one reason why so many startup companies, as well as products and services offered by larger firms, fail.

Some Better Mousetraps

Marketing strategy begins with the identification of customer need or want. It is only then that attention turns to advertising, personal selling, pricing, and distribution. Often, someone with a product or service will ask a marketer to sell it without first determining whether there is a need or want. That is putting the cart before the horse.

Snowing Yourself

Anyone who has devoted a considerable amount of time to developing a technology or product is likely to become enamored of it. This is true whether we are talking about an inventor working out of a garage or an R&D group using the modern laboratory facilities of a major corporation. Therein lies the danger—a loss of objectivity about the realistic prospects for the product in the marketplace.

Suga Test Instruments Company of Tokyo is Japan's leading manufacturer of environmental testing equipment. Suga invested over $4 million and five years of time in developing a machine capable of making various kinds of snow precisely in a laboratory. The snowmaking machines used on ski slopes do not yield genuine snow, just ice, and snowmaking in laboratories cannot offer the versatility of the Suga equipment. Suga's high-tech snowmaking machine can reproduce twenty-seven of the nearly five hundred types of snow crystals at the rate of about one foot every twenty-four hours.

Suga's management believed that this snow machine would be needed by automobile companies to test car parts and accessories under wintertime conditions. Supposedly, the auto companies would subject windshield-wiper blades, radiators, and power cables to machine-made snow. Apparel companies such as London Fog, L.L. Bean, and Descente were thought to be prospects for the snow machine, in addition to large-scale clothing purchasers like the U.S. military. Public utilities might be interested in testing their power lines.

Suga priced the snowmaking marvel at $1.3 million a unit and sold none. The automobile companies were not interested because snow is not what they are concerned about. One worry is with what happens to wiper blades and parts after the snow melts and mixes with contaminants; other worries are heat and cold. Not snow. The apparel companies and the U.S. military gauge the durability of clothing and outdoor gear by field-testing it under actual conditions and by dressing a copper dummy and putting it in a climatic chamber. Public utilities test power lines by stringing them up outside during the winter. And the Battelle Memorial Institute in Columbus, Ohio, has been developing a robot that will test clothing for the U.S. Army by crawling, painting, and sweating.

Poor Timing

Texas Instruments (TI) is an engineering-oriented, R&D-driven company that has had numerous successes in selling to high-tech companies and the U.S. government. In its specialties, TI is a premier company.

But TI's attempt to expand its technological know-how into consumer goods was a disaster. Being able to build better mousetraps to specifications for other companies and the military did not qualify TI to deal with the additional twists and turns of consumer-goods marketing.

TI tried to gain a leadership position in the then-infant digital watch industry. Without a doubt, TI had the technological knowhow to produce a superior digital watch. One of its products was a joggers' watch. In addition to keeping time, the watch had a stopwatch capability. But incredibly, the stopwatch function would recycle every fifteen minutes, forcing the jogger to keep mental track of how many fifteen-minute increments had elapsed. A serious jogger who ran five or six or more increments a day could easily lose track of the elapsed time. Not surprisingly, Casio, Timex, and others won the market with a comparably priced watch entailing a regular time feature, a stopwatch capacity of up to eleven hours and fifty-nine minutes, a light for telling time in the dark, and almost any other bell and whistle imaginable for a watch.

Later, a similar sad story was repeated by TI with in-home personal computers, causing a loss that prompted TI's withdrawal from the in-home market and a precipitous one-day drop in the price of the company's common stock. The company's reputation has never fully recovered from these debacles in watches and computers.

Disc What the Customer Did Not Order

Early in 1981, with great fanfare, RCA introduced its version of a videodisc player, SelectaVision. RCA billed videodiscs as a technology that would "revolutionize" the home entertainment industry. One of its advertisements trumpeted that RCA was introducing the most stirring entertainment innovation since television itself. Its competitors made equally optimistic claims. RCA had ten years of R&D time and resources invested in the videodisc player and committed massive marketing expenditures to sell it. J.C. Penney and Montgomery Ward signed on to distribute RCA's videodisc player, and Sears, Roebuck offered it under its own brand in its 1981 Christmas catalogue.

A videodisc is akin to a phonograph that can also show pictures. The videodisc player is attached to a television. The prerecorded disc is placed in the disc player and then played on the television set, just as a record is played on a stereo. People could buy discs of movies, sports events, arts, and children's programs. Businesses and educational institutions could use "how-to" discs as teaching and training devices. Popular features offered by manufacturers included fast motion, slow motion, and stop motion.

Magnavox introduced the videodisc technology into the United States in 1978. There were a number of domestic and foreign competitors in the videodisc market selling four incompatible technologies.

This incompatibility promised to create exactly the same problem that Sony encountered with its Betamax videocassette recorders (VCRs). Sony's Betamax VCRs would not play the far more popular VHS tapes, which finally forced Sony to develop a VHS player and, in effect, abandon its Betamax, at least for consumer markets. In the case of videodiscs, the customer ran the risk of buying one manufacturer's technology, only to have another manufacturer's technology ultimately prevail. Then the customer would not be able to obtain new discs for his now-obsolete videodisc player.

RCA was so ebullient about the prospects for its videodisc player and the market potential for the technology that the company termed it the Manhattan Project, the same name used by the United States to develop the atomic bomb. Reality set in about late 1981 when RCA's videodisc registered extremely disappointing sales figures for the Christmas season. RCA struggled along until 1984, when it withdrew from the videodisc market with reported losses of $580 million. It was not alone. Indeed, the videodisc player market in the United States was effectively dead.

RCA's then-chairman and chief executive officer, Thornton F. Bradshaw, commented that the videodisc player was "a technological success but a commercial failure." But people buy solutions to their problems and desires, not technological successes, and the solution in this instance is the now-ubiquitous VCR.

RCA had believed that its videodisc player would be able to compete with the rival VCR technology. Why? Because the videodisc players were less expensive than and not as complicated to operate as VCRs. Almost $600 million was lost on this reasoning. The fact is, RCA management was so enamored of the videodisc technology that it had grasped at virtually any reason to continue its R&D effort—its own Manhattan Project. After all, videodiscs would be the best thing to happen to the entertainment business since television, and RCA had pioneered that medium.

The videodisc player never had a chance against VCRs in the United States for one decisive reason, a reason that it takes no marketing research at all to uncover: the videodisc player did not have a recording capability, and the VCR does. That is all there was to it! A VCR owner could record a movie, sports event, or whatever on network television and cable channels for the price of a VCR tape. The unfortunate owner of a videodisc player first had to search for a disc compatible with his or her player, mindful that there were four competing technologies. Once a technologically compatible disc was located, there was a limited disc selection from which to choose. RCA offered only 150 titles. Finally, the purchase price for a disc ranged from $15 to $25.

Would most consumers opt for the videodisc solution or the one offered by the VCR? RCA spent millions and its reputation betting on the videodisc; no telling how much its competitors spent. The point is that the videodisc player was not a good risk because the VCR technology was already available by the early 1980s for everyone to see. And the VCR's recording capability was devastating —a knockout factor if there ever was one.

Why Bother?

Eureka! A major appliance maker had an idea for a refrigerator with a see-through door. The company developed a prototype and took it to a consumer trade show. But that was the end of the line: A see-through front means no shelf space in the door and that visitors can readily view a messy interior.

Given these two compelling reasons why someone would not purchase a see-through refrigerator, it is hard to conceive of even one reason why someone *would* purchase one. The rationale behind the development of this masterpiece mousetrap was that the refrigerator allowed household members to assess their supply of milk, mayonnaise, and other staples without opening the door and using extra electricity.

A consumer research study that consisted of talking with several refrigerator owners and grocery shoppers for about five minutes each would have saved the time and money that went into the R&D effort. But no study was made, which shows the danger of developing and commercializing new ventures without talking initially, in the idea stage, to people who are targeted as customers.

A Better Mousetrap?

When Emerson remarked that if you built a better mousetrap, the world would beat a path to your door, he was speaking figuratively.

But take him literally and see where this building-better-mousetrap thinking can lead.

Several years ago, I left a basement window open, and a mouse accepted what he apparently thought was my invitation to enter. This invader rummaged and scratched around the basement at night and during the early morning hours. I called in one of those exterminating firms that so boldly advertise their pest-killing prowess in the yellow pages. Their technician arrived at my house looking like someone on the cover of those soldier of fortune magazines, and he acted the same way—kind of a Johnny Rambo of the rodent and insect world. He clinically went about the task at hand. He placed his lethal pellets, warned me to keep children and pets away, confidently assured me of the mouse's impending demise, and handed me a healthy bill for services rendered. Then he sort of swaggered off to his truck. We were sure that the mouse was spending his last day with us. Yes, indeed.

It did not work. The mouse survived beautifully. As a last resort—which should have been my first resort—for less than a dollar I purchased the familiar mousetrap with the wire-wood-cheese technology that people have been using for no telling how long. I set it—and it worked that very day.

Now, compare this wire-wood-cheese mousetrap to a more technologically sophisticated one. The advanced model lures the unsuspecting mouse with the scent of the opposite sex. Both male and female scents are used for bait, so that one does not have to guess the mouse's gender before setting the trap. When the mouse enters the trap, say at 2:30 A.M., the trap closes and electrocutes the mouse, which dies happy. A music box in the trap's innards triumphantly plays Tchaikovsky's *1812 Overture* to alert the masters of the household.

There is more. The household residents, having been alerted by the music, are able to see, via the television monitor in their bedroom hooked to the in-house cable system, that the "kill" has been made in the living room. They are ecstatic—their better mousetrap has performed as the manufacturer promised it would. Well done, indeed.

However, there is one small consideration. The new-improved mousetrap is technological "overkill," so to speak. Like Suga Test's snowmaking machine, no reasonable person would pay the price for it.

This better-mousetrap technology is based on a system used on some Thoroughbred race-horse farms for security purposes. The farm might "wire" the paddock of a valuable stallion by placing sensing devices under the ground around the paddock's perimeter. The sensors can be calibrated so that a rabbit or small dog crossing the paddock will not set off the alarm. For instance, the system could be programmed so that an animal would have to weigh sixty-five pounds before triggering the sensors.

Consider an actual incident to see how the system works. A stallion in his paddock knocked down the top board in one section of the wooden fence. When he tried to escape, the alarm registered on a television screen in a guard house, showing in which paddock specifically there was trouble. The security guard monitoring the television then acted before the stallion departed to a nearby road. In this case, the better mousetrap was worth the money necessary to buy it.

People do not purchase products, services, or technologies per se. Rather, they seek solutions to their needs and wants. What they are willing to pay for these solutions must be commensurate with the magnitude of their needs and wants. Buying a $2,500 security system for a valuable stallion's paddock is one thing; buying it to catch mice is another. This cost-versus-benefit comparison seems obvious. Yet why are consumers offered $1.3 million snow-making machines, runners' stopwatches that time for a mere fifteen minutes, videodiscs that do not record, and a host of other such products and services? The answer is that the people in the companies that developed them became so involved that they were unwilling or unable to ask the tough questions and act on unwanted answers.

Blind Mice

Ford Motor Company's consumer research clearly indicated that Edsel was a poor name for a car. Someone's decision to name one of the legendary losers in commercial history after the company founder's only son must have been haunting.

Another example: A market research study done in connection with a new shopping center indicated that a particular name for the center should not be selected. Surprise! Surprise! The name was selected because top management liked the name so well that the brochures for prospective tenants and news releases for the media had already been printed. What is more, the market researcher who tested possible names for the new shopping center was criticized by his immediate boss for doing so. Once the steamroller effect of building a better mousetrap is in full motion, it is difficult for objectivity to change its course or to slow it down.

"Stay the Course" or "Cut the Losses"?

Today as a group, FM radio stations are generally hotter properties than AM stations. This is a remarkable reversal of the situation only a few years ago, when AM stations were king. What propelled FM to the forefront was its stereo capability. As all-music stations became increasingly popular, listeners switched to FM to obtain better-quality sound transmission.

Fighting back, AM stations too began to acquire the technology to broadcast in stereo. However, most radios do not have the capability to receive AM stereo, and therein lies the problem.

Here is a competitive situation that will take years to right itself. AM will not be competing on a level playing field with FM until well into the next century. AM's situation relative to FM depends on the answer to one key question: How long does a radio last? Many of the radios now in use with FM stereo capability will be around for a long time. Is there anything that AM stereo stations can do to change things? Probably not, short of giving away radios with AM stereo. Although AM stereo is far superior to AM without stereo, most people are not about to "beat a path" to a retailer to purchase a radio to receive it. Consumers already have the option of receiving FM stereo without spending the money for a new radio. Stereo television faces a similar problem. People have not flocked to buy television sets with stereo sound; the older but "already-paid-for" nonstereo televisions will do just fine for now.

AM stereo will eventually be commonplace one day. It is not a commercial dud doomed to permanent rejection in the marketplace. But its acceptance will be slow in coming. So even if a company builds a better product or offers a better service, like stereo AM, prospective buyers are not always impressed enough to purchase quickly. Consumers usually take their time in making up their minds, especially for big-ticket items.

History clearly teaches that new ideas and innovations can take as little as eight to twelve weeks to become widely accepted, as in the case of hula hoops. Twenty-five million were sold in the spring and summer of 1958. Other ideas take one hundred years or more to catch on, such as audiovisual equipment in public school systems. Transistors did not immediately replace bulky vacuum tubes, diesel-electric engines took time to phase out steam locomotives, jet engines continue to coexist with aircraft propellers, black and white televisions are still available, and antiquated farm equipment is the choice of Amish farmers. George Eastman sold only ten thousand of his first Kodak cameras in 1888, which retailed for $25, whereas he sold 750,000 Brownie cameras in their first year on the market in 1900.

Most entrepreneurs of new products and services eventually face the decision of whether to stay the course or cut the losses. Rarely does a new venture gain immediate commercial acceptance and relieve the entrepreneur of this continue/abort decision. A basic question becomes, Is there a fundamental product or service defect accounting for our slow sales, or do we have a useful concept that will only take time to sell? Will time and additional marketing turn the tide for us?

It is difficult to give up on a product or service with which a person has high personal involvement. But often it is a necessary business decision. Sometimes the only thing that a product or service will realistically achieve with more time and additional effort is age.

From 1963 to 1971, Du Pont Corporation spent perhaps $100 million on developing, manufacturing, and marketing their leather substitute called Corfam. When Corfam was introduced, Du Pont sang its praises as though it were another Nylon. The company later changed its tune and ultimately sang the blues. Du Pont called it quits with Corfam in 1971. Ever since, its top managers have used the product as a painful and personal illustration to Du Pont executives and technical people of the dangers of the building-better-mousetraps school of thought. Du Pont had had consumer research that warned of critical problems with Corfam as a leather substitute in shoes. But Du Pont executives apparently were not alarmed that many consumers in a product test considered a Corfam-made shoe to be uncomfortable. They also were unfazed that high-quality shoe manufacturers like Florsheim uncompromisingly stipulated in corporate policy that all shoes in their line would be leather.

The vast majority of people and companies do not have deep pockets to cover their mistakes. Another important question is whether the entrepreneur has the time, money, and patience to stay the course and suffer the consequences should they be bad. King Gillette's safety razors and blades did not gain widespread use until World War I, when U.S. soldiers on duty began shaving themselves daily and the military purchased over four million Gillette safety razors. The discharged doughboys and their comrades in arms took the habit of frequently shaving home with them at war's end, and their preferred brand of razor and blade was Gillette.

Harland Sanders is another case of entrepreneurial perseverance against long odds. The honorary colonel from southern Indiana worked at various nondescript jobs for years. He struggled most of his life. Eventually, he moved to Corbin, Kentucky, where he opened a restaurant and perfected his recipe for Kentucky Fried Chicken. This restaurant was effectively put out of business by a four-lane highway that bypassed it, leaving the "Colonel" an out-of-work sixty-six-year-old with nothing to live on but a small Social Security pension. Should he continue on with his secret recipe? This kind of decision is why entrepreneurship is generally for the young. Unlike most entrepreneurs and companies with new ventures, Colonel Sanders made it.

Harland Sanders and King Gillette happened to be right in their convictions about the commercial feasibility of their products. But whether it is a down-on-his-luck sixty-six-year-old erstwhile restaurateur like Harland Sanders, or an inventor and peddler like King Gillette, or the prestigious Du Pont or RCA, there is a natural susceptibility to fall prey to the better-mousetrap trap. It is a gripping feeling, sometimes a euphoria, that causes all kinds of symptoms, the potentially most devastating being the loss of objectivity in evaluating whether to continue on or to call it a day.

Over a decade ago, I purchased some residential lots in the far suburbs of a large city. Ever since then, I have held them in the hopes that people will "come to their senses" and buy these "beautiful lots" to build their houses on, naturally at a nice profit for me. I glossed over the three principles of evaluating real estate—location, location, location—and, as a result, I am now cutting my losses on my own mousetraps.

Is the Mousetrap Philosophy Ever Right?

Sure. Innovations such as the telephone, the automobile, the airplane, and the polio vaccine were so revolutionary and so exciting and fulfilled people's needs and desires so well that they initially sold themselves. In the early 1900s, a grateful farm woman wrote to Henry Ford and thanked him for getting her out of the mud with the Model T. Ford's innovation changed the world. His automobiles met such basic needs for personal mobility that, for a time, people beat a path to his door.

In the 1950s, polio was so feared that most parents took all kinds of precautions against it. Children were not allowed to swim in creeks or ponds. Visits to towns with epidemic outbreaks of polio were avoided. When Jonas Salk discovered the first successful poliomyelitis vaccine, there was great relief. Once the Salk vaccine was commercialized, little more than an announcement was needed to sell it. But even in this case of life and death, public health officials had to work hard to get some segments of the population vaccinated.

A cure for any type of cancer would not require much marketing. Upjohn's treatment for male pattern baldness and Merck's drug to reduce cholesterol also promise strong consumer demand without intensive marketing. When their patent protection runs out, however, marketing will be very important.

To the extent that a product or service revolutionizes the way we work and live as a society or to the extent that it fulfills a basic human need or desire, it does not need bold marketing. A developer of a drug to treat dwarfism received inquiries from parents of normal-size children. These parents wanted to promote additional growth in their offspring, particularly in boys, apparently mostly for athletic reasons—seven-footers get college scholarships and NBA contracts. Similarly, an effective treatment for the deadly AIDS virus would literally bring an onslaught of desperate people to the developer's door. New and exciting discoveries from fields like biotechnology or gene-splicing will open up entire markets that do not even exist today.

However, these products are few and far between. The U.S. Patent and Trademark Office has patented countless inventions over the years, but most of them have no demonstrable or probable commercial value. Yet hope springs eternal. Recently, a patent was issued on a flag-waving machine—it moves a flag in a figure-eight pattern and holds it in an outstretched position, as if the flag were in a stiff breeze. A sensor was patented that informs a golfer of excessive head movement during his or her swing. Then there is a radio antenna that is supposed to be able to survive a nuclear blast.

One day an inventor who wanted to manufacture and sell coverings for shoes came to see me. On Sunday, he said, you could wear black, on Monday brown, and so on as your tastes dictated. Think of the money you could save by only having to buy one pair of shoes. He was sold on his own product, and consequently did not think much of my suggestion that people alternate shoes for sanitary as well as for aesthetic reasons. When I told him the coverings looked, let us say, inexpensive, he really winced. But when he left my office, he was undaunted by my critique and was on his way to a fashion-goods distributor for another opinion.

In-home shopping via a personal computer and a modem (for nonusers of computers, a modem is a device that links computers by phone) was reputed by many "experts" to be a "can't miss" proposition. Consumers would browse through electronic catalogues of goods, like an electronic mall, and then order their selections by using their personal computers to instruct the shopping service's centrally located computer. Some established companies—Reader's Digest, Times Mirror, CBS, Knight-Ridder, and CompuServe—invested in this videotex venture. But it has been a commercial failure. Either the idea is ahead of its time, or it is ill conceived. Most Americans do not have personal computers and modems. Consumers prefer the familiar, which is offered by in-person shopping, where the merchandise can be observed and handled, or by direct purchasing via the familiar mail or phone. In addition, in-home television shopping has also come along; there all the consumer needs is a TV, a telephone, and a credit card.

Without a doubt, most new technologies, processes, products, and services are not revolutionary and earthshaking in the sense that they radically change the way we live and work. The few that are encourage building-better-mousetrap thinking, which focuses on what a technology or product offers rather than on what buyers want. The *New York Times* annual edition of the *World Almanac* usually devotes only four or five pages to listing the most notable inventions and discoveries of all mankind since as far back as the 1600s. But now in just one year alone, over 75,000 patents are registered in the United States. How many pages would *all* worldwide inventions and discoveries since 1600 take up? How many were truly revolutionary?

In 1947, Howard Hughes flew the Hughes H$_4$ Hercules, known as the *Spruce Goose,* for one mile over Los Angeles harbor at a height of eighty feet. The *Spruce Goose* was the largest flying boat in the world—also the largest airplane ever flown, and the aircraft with the greatest wingspan ever built. It could hold up to seven hundred passengers. It was its first and last trip. Today a museum piece, it may stand as the largest monument ever to where the mousetrap philosophy can lead in the name of R&D.

Can You Listen to Customers Too Closely?

As a marketer, you cannot listen to customers too closely. How customers feel about the products and services a company offers is enormously important in maintaining a high level of customer satisfaction. Furthermore, suggestions for product and service improvements can be garnered from asking customers to voice their problems and needs.

However, listening to customers *closely* does not mean listening to them *exclusively.* Market development requires that firms seek out noncustomers as well, to see what might be done about turning them into customers. And innovation demands that companies seek advice and ideas on meeting customer needs from a variety of sources—for instance, R&D people, engineers, sales reps, assembly-line employees, and secretaries. Imagine a buggy whip manufacturer of around 1900 who listened only to his customers. Imagine that his customers told the manufacturer he was doing a fine job but suggested a slight increase in the leather quality to improve durability. Making that improvement and thus catering to his customers would not have saved him from the industry's inevitable decline. A far more innovative diversification would have been needed, and the livery stable operator, the carriage maker, and the buckboard driver would hardly be the right people to ask about what course that diversification might take.

Evaluating Products, Services, and Ventures

When an entrepreneur assesses the feasibility of launching a new product, a new service, or even a new business, he or she is in one of several situations regarding the amount of evidence to support going ahead.

• *There is no market research at all; the entrepreneur is acting mainly on instinct and intuition.* This is often the case in small businesses because the entrepreneur cannot or will not fund a market feasibility study.

• *Information about market potential exists, but its accuracy, reliability, or relevance is in question.* For instance, the information may be based on small, unrepresentative samples, or it may be outdated.

• *A credible and relevant information base exists.* This base is the result of the work of knowledgeable and reputable market researchers who are adept at the ins and outs of questionnaire design, statistical sampling, data analysis, and other elements of professional consumer research.

• *Market research exists, but there is no analysis available of likely competitors.* A thorough competitor analysis might find that even though a product fulfills a customer need or want, it does not fulfill the need as well as a competitive technology.

• *Well-researched information is available both on market potential and on actual and possible competitors.* This is the ideal situation.

Entrepreneurial risk is greatest when decisions are made on intuition alone or on poorly conducted market research. Yes, many examples can be found of products and businesses that were launched on instinct and turned out to be magnificent successes. Roy Rowan of *Fortune* magazine wrote a much-needed book, *The Intuitive Manager,* that discusses the power of insight, hunch, and "gut feeling" in business, sports, and other human endeavors. What I call canny intuition flows from observation and experience and allows one to speculate about the future. It is a rudimentary form of market research and is especially helpful in generating ideas— for new products, services, businesses, and markets—that can be tested more thoroughly by conventional means. Innovative solutions to consumers' problems and desires spring from observation and speculation.

Entrepreneurial risk is reduced by appropriate market research and a thorough analysis of current and possible competition. Even here, however, the entrepreneur may be tempted to ignore or skim over results that augur poorly for the project at hand. The Ford Motor Company named its car Edsel in spite of the red flag from its own consumer research, and Du Pont plunged into the manufacturing of Corfam for shoes even though its consumer studies revealed significant comfort problems.

Few companies face more uncertainty in commercializing new products than those in biotechnology. Plant Genetics of Davis, California, was founded in 1981, and quickly became a leader in agricultural biotechnology. It develops and sells genetically improved crops such as potatoes, alfalfa, and tomatoes. Zachary Wochok, the company's president, says that at Plant Genetics, senior management's attitude toward marketing researchers is, "Tell us what we can do in sales and share with a new product, not what we want to hear." An objective assessment of market potential is what Wochok wants, regardless of the outcome.

Questions to Ask Yourself

1. Are you acting on canny intuition alone? If so, are you being penny wise and pound foolish by not commissioning an independent (for objectivity) and reputable person or firm to analyze the market and competition?

2. Do you have hard evidence indicating that your proposed business venture will achieve the financial and market objectives you have in mind? Have you set clear objectives in concrete terms such as market share, growth, and return on investment?

3. Have you solicited "expert opinion" from people who are knowledgeable about your industry and product line? As an experienced racetrack executive once commented on the rapid commercial failure of the Birmingham Turf Club in Alabama, "I could have told them that would happen for the price of two drinks."

4. How many potential customers have you personally talked to in person and in depth about their needs, preferences, and problems, and about how your product or service might be helpful? Did you ask them about the competition? Given a choice between your offering and what is being offered by the competition, which would the customer prefer?

5. Are you looking at the evidence you have in hand in an objective way, or have you let your involvement with the product or service cloud your vision? What does your market research say? What does your outside counsel—the experts and potential customers you have asked—tell you? Are you about to market your product because it fulfills a customer need or want better than the competition (the right reason), or simply because you have something to sell (the wrong reason)? Have you identified a customer need in want of a better solution, or do you have a product or service in search of an application?

6. If a Las Vegas casino were to take your bet, what odds would you want before wagering your house or job on the success of your proposed venture in the commercial marketplace? If you want more than 3-1, something concerns you a great deal about the venture's commercial feasibility.

3
Blunder #2:
Selling Too Much Sizzle,
Not Enough Steak

It's a lot easier to differentiate your product through the quality of the marketing than through the quality of the product. . . . It is easier to change your advertising campaign than it is to build a better car.
—James Koch, chief executive officer of the Boston Beer Company

In the early days of the mass-production economy, products were sold mainly for utilitarian reasons. The emphasis was on the physical need that a product was intended to satisfy rather than on the psychological satisfactions it provided. The refrigerator model that replaced the icebox was sold on its ability to keep food and beverages cold, not on its style, color, or other aesthetic considerations. Later, as competition intensified and consumers became more selective, companies began to differentiate their offerings by catering to unmet psychological needs.

In many companies, the thinking eventually took hold that products and services are basically commodities. One company's product or service was just about like another's. Therefore, what sold them was not so much the quality of the commodity as the quality of the marketing. Then the Japanese came along and proved otherwise. They competed *both* with aggressive and creative marketing that appealed to psychological needs *and* with quality products that delivered on their promises.

There is no doubt whatsoever that people derive physical and psychological satisfaction from many of the products and services they buy. Not all, but most. Industrial products, of course, are bought more for utilitarian reasons than consumer products are, but psychological considerations come into play even with industrial products. When companies begin to lose sight of the bundle of physical, intangible, and psychological attributes that they are offering to potential customers, they are on the road to failure. They will experience difficulty in selling their offerings for one of two reasons: Either they have a high-quality product or service but a drab, unexciting marketing program that neglects important psychological appeals; or, more likely, they deploy an exciting marketing program that has the right psychology but delivers a product or service that does not measure up to customers' quality expectations. This latter case is described by the metaphor about selling too much sizzle but not enough steak.

Say What? "Hot Buttons for the Quality Vector"?

A year after James Koch founded the Boston Beer Company, he was asked to address the new-ventures club at the Harvard School of Business. Koch describes the experience:

> I began by telling my audience that our biggest challenge as a startup was creating in the customer's mind an image of quality. "Okay," I said, "what do you think we should have done first?" Hands went up all over the room. "The first thing you do is get some good market research," one said. "Hire an ad agency," said another. "Find a good public relations firm," offered a third. One person actually said something about convening focus groups so we could "locate the hot buttons for the quality vector." The hot buttons for the quality vector? What the hell is *that* supposed to mean? As if quality were something that existed independent of the beer itself.
>
> Nobody—not one of them—said something on the order of, "If you're trying to create an image in consumers' minds of a better beer, the first thing you do is brew a better beer." Then it was *my* turn to get riled. I told them this was a perfect example of where American business is today: looking to sell me-too products through better marketing. And I also said, "Look, in my business you have only two ways of surviving: either your product is better than your competitors', or it's cheaper. There's simply no other foundation on which to build a successful business. None. Better or cheaper—take your pick."

Today, chastened by the Japanese and other tough competitors, top managers in companies of all sizes know, like James Koch, that effective business strategy requires both quality offerings and aggressive marketing—both the steak and the sizzle. But effective strategy begins with the steak.

The Quality Ethic

The best way to describe Pat Ailes is as a craftsman of the old school of doing things. Shirley Betkoski is a teacher who demands that her students learn the three R's. As John Houseman would have said, they make money the old-fashioned way—they earn it. We have all met someone like them.

Pat Ailes, who builds and remodels houses, produces the type of work that you see illustrated in the shelter and architectural magazines. He is an artisan, and he crafts for his customers quality, aesthetics, and satisfaction. If you were to call him, he might be a long time getting to your job. His quality work sells well.

Shirley Betkoski teaches the fourth grade. No students pass through her class perfunctorily on the way to the fifth grade. She cares. Regardless of a child's intellectual capability, he or she works up to capacity. Shirley has won no popularity contests, no "teacher of the year" awards, but her "products," the children, are quality— they can read, write, and do arithmetic. What important characteristics these are. The Japanese threaten the United States economically and technologically partly because of their educational system, which fills the Japanese work force with literate and scientifically knowledgeable young people with a strong work ethic.

Quality-providers like Pat and Shirley labor in relative obscurity in every occupation, sometimes unappreciated—or even scorned. Fast workers on assembly lines are sometimes referred to pejoratively by co-workers as "rate busters." Abraham Lincoln—a quality president—was in his time called everything from "half-witted" to an "obscene clown" to "the craftiest and most dishonest politician that ever disgraced an office in America."

It is usually the quality-achievers who rise to the top of their lines of work and sometimes gain fame. Susan Lombardi, daughter of the legendary professional football coach Vince Lombardi, has told me many times of her father's dedication to excellence in life's undertakings per se, not just in the profession for which he is remembered. Long before Vince Lombardi was immortalized in the annals of sports history, he was giving quality instruction in a number of scholastic subjects to students at St. Cecelia High in Englewood, New Jersey, where he coached basketball and football. Lombardi lived his credo that "you don't do things right once in a while, you do them right all the time." This disciplined approach to one's life work was no doubt ingrained in Lombardi by another legendary football coach, Colonel "Red" Blake of the U.S. Military Academy, for whom Lombardi once worked as an assistant. People like Max McGee and Willie Davis, who were Green Bay Packers during the dynasty years and are now wealthy entrepreneurs, are quick to credit Coach Lombardi for instilling in them the commitment to excellence that has served them so well in the business world.

Quality work does not guarantee someone or some company success and prosperity. However, quality products and services are almost always prerequisites to lasting or sustained success in the commercial marketplace. This has been true for centuries, for the butcher, the baker, and the candlestick maker. It continues to be true for the individual, the small or medium-size business, and the global company. And it will be increasingly so in the years ahead, as competition intensifies. A Hart, Schaffner & Marx advertisement for executives' suits says that the clothes you wear cannot get you into the corporate boardroom, but they can keep you out. This philosophy also applies to quality: a company's high-quality products and services do not assure commercial success, but low-quality products sooner or later result in failure.

Fowl Quality

If I were asked to pick one company that I think is the model for what it takes to compete today, my choice would be Perdue Farms of Salisbury, Maryland. Frank Perdue built his family's small chicken-producing operation into the fifth-largest company in its industry. He achieved this growth by combining a zeal for quality with aggressive and innovative marketing.

Few products are more of a commodity than chickens. One person's chickens are about like the next person's. So the only alternative is to compete on price. That was the way most people saw things before 1971. Few chicken producers, maybe none, had ever advertised chickens before, much less built a creative campaign around superior product quality.

The cornerstone of Perdue's business strategy is a quality offering. He begins with a crossbreed of leghorns and Cornish chickens that his scientists have perfected for fast growth and meatiness. This genetic potential is realized by feeding the birds a mixture of soybeans, vitamins, proteins, and minerals that a flock of Perdue's R&D people are constantly trying to improve. To add the right amount of sizzle, the chickens are also fed marigold leaves to turn their skins bright yellow. This color distinguishes Perdue chickens and appeals to consumers. After being raised in squeaky-clean environments, the chickens are processed in equally clean plants. During processing, chickens that do not meet lofty Perdue standards are rejected by quality-control personnel. The chickens that do pass inspection are shipped to market in packages with a red flag—a Perdue symbol of quality. This meticulous attention to quality and cleanliness becomes the basis for marketing and promotion. In turn, Perdue chickens command premium prices in the supermarkets.

Frank Perdue is personally and professionally a perfectionist—whether he is taking a walk at a precise 12.5-minute pace per mile, having the American flag raised and lowered at corporate headquarters at the correct time, or producing and marketing chickens. He has taken this quality orientation, this attention to detail, this crossing the t's and dotting the i's, and combined them with bold marketing and promotion that have just the right amount of sizzle.

A chicken company from a small town in Maryland is an unlikely candidate as an exemplar of effective market strategy. But look everywhere—from high-tech to low-tech firms, from industry giants to one-person operations—and try to find a more deserving candidate.

"The Loneliest Man In Town"

The American Marketing Association once sponsored a conference billed as Quality and the Customer. One of the presentations—"Key Issues for Success with Quality and the Customer"—was by

Daniel J. Krumm, chairman and chief executive officer of the Maytag Company of Newton, Iowa. How appropriate—who better to talk on quality? Maytag is consistently rated in consumer and product tests as the crème de la crème maker of washers and dryers. Their sad-looking repairman is widely known from Maytag's print and television advertising as "the loneliest man in town." Maytag, probably more than any single company, has demonstrated that quality sells in the marketplace.

Another speaker at the same conference was James Petrie, managing director of customer service for Federal Express. Again, how suitable. Tom Peters, best known as the co-author of *In Search of Excellence,* once described on television how he put Federal Express to his own rigorous customer service test. Secluded on his New England farm while writing a book, Peters regularly needed to send materials to his secretary on the West Coast. He called Federal Express twenty-seven times. On twenty-six of those calls, he was answered on the first ring. The one time his call was not answered on the first ring, he was so surprised that he hung up and called right back: Federal Express answered on the first ring. Peters said he might have dialed the wrong number the other time.

After hearing Peters tell this anecdote, I began using Federal Express. My experience has been the same as his—they really do answer right away. I also have never had a complaint with my own Maytag washer and dryer, and I hope to keep contributing to the Maytag repairman's sense of isolation.

The Maytags, the Perdue Farms, and the Federal Expresses of the world have been eminently successful in taking the quality ethic adhered to by the one-person quality-purveyors—like woodcraftsman Pat Ailes and schoolteacher Shirley Betkoski—and ingraining it into a large organization. Other organizations have seen that quality is a potent competitive weapon and are trying their best to build and sell better-quality products or to provide higher-quality services. A voice-over on a John Deere ad asks a kindly-looking elderly farmer, "How long does a John Deere last?" After the farmer contemplates the question awhile, he repeats the question and ponders the answer. Obviously coming up blank, he replies, "That's a good question." End of ad.

Everyone's Got a Horror Story

Try an experiment. Jot down every unpleasant experience that you personally have had as a consumer in connection with products and services you bought or attempted to buy. My own list would be several healthy paragraphs long. Most adults would have little difficulty in quickly reeling off a litany of rude, cavalier, or uninformed salespeople, misleading or outright fraudulent sales presentations, unresponsive companies, belligerent secretaries or receptionists, lemons that did not work from day one, warranties that were disregarded, "easy-to-assemble" products that required a technician to put together, and just plain ripoffs.

Pierre Rinfret, a renowned economist, is the president of Rinfret Associates in New York City, an international economic, financial, and political intelligence organization. He has advised U.S. Presidents on economic and competitive issues and is on the boards of directors of five major corporations. He is a crusader for better quality offerings by U.S. companies. Rinfret holds strong views about the quality issue and what it means in terms of global competitiveness for the United States. He believes that the Japanese have done us an enormous favor as a nation: "We Americans got fat, dumb, and happy. It took the Japanese to teach us that quality is not a thing of the past, that warranties are something to be honored, that competition exists and is real in this world."

As part of his call for U.S. businesses to meet the competitive challenge of providing higher-quality products and services, Rinfret enumerates his own personal list of horrors:

> a brand-new car that breaks down five blocks from the showroom; a brand-new freezer that won't start; a new shoe whose heel drops off two blocks from the retail store; a new computer, made by an eminent firm, that won't even switch on; bottles of soda that contain every kind of filth imaginable; a shotgun without firing pins; an air conditioner that doesn't cool the air; and a car that was supposedly "repaired" but actually wasn't.
>
> How about a painter who spills paint all over the floor and, when asked how it happened, says, "Who knows? Why does it matter?"; a plumber who destroys more than he fixes; a carpenter who nails chair guard rails to the wall and they fall off after

he leaves; a cleaner who brings back (and hangs) draperies that he forgot to clean; an airline ticket agent who refuses to tag your luggage; a retail sales clerk who's talking to other clerks but who tells you she is busy when you ask for service; a policeman who tells you to pay a ticket because "you rich bastards can afford it!"; an airline stewardess who tells you to find your own blanket; an insurance company executive who tells you that you're lucky you can even get insurance (it was regular major medical insurance).

Also on the list of horrors. How about a bowling ball made of a plastic that softens when it's left in the trunk of your car; a fishing rod that breaks the first time you use it; a spinning reel that doesn't spin; airline employees who loudly denigrate their passengers; airline personnel who send your luggage to Tokyo instead of Chicago; bolts that won't fit the nuts supplied with them; a soldering iron that doesn't heat; red paint in a can marked "white"; retail goods that are marked up and then put on "sale" with a sale price that is the standard retail price; the department store clerks who tell you their computers are never wrong; the credit card company that cancels your card for unknown reasons and then wants you to pay a renewal fee; the package of meat whose underside is hidden when you buy it and turns out to be all fat and bone when unwrapped; the laborer who submits a bill for phony hours; the consultant who visits two clients in the same area on the same trip but charges each of them full travel expenses; the lawyer who inflates his billable hours; the accountant who makes a major mistake on your tax return and charges you for correcting it.

I was anxious to see if Pierre Rinfret's firm really practices what its founder preaches about quality. So I called the New York office of Rinfret Associates to ask if I could include some of Dr. Rinfret's writings and thoughts in this book. First, I was answered in a businesslike and cordial manner by the receptionist. Then I was transferred to Rinfret's assistant, who was helpful and polite far beyond my expectations. She asked me to write to Rinfret with my request. He received my letter on a Tuesday and called me back the very next day. I was not in, but I returned his call and was put right through. We talked for half an hour about the quality issue and what it means for U.S. global competitiveness and the domestic economy in the coming years. Yes, my experience with

Rinfret Associates confirmed that the firm goes out of its way to be helpful, and I was not even a client.

Contrast the treatment this service firm accorded to me with an experience my wife, Joan, had on a Florida-to-Ohio flight on one of the well-known airlines. Her plane from Jacksonville to Atlanta was late, but in Atlanta the airline would not hold the connecting flight to Cleveland for another five minutes. The next flight to Cleveland left at dawn, so she had to spend the night in Atlanta. One of the airline's ticket agents handed her a list of area motels. Joan asked the agent where they were located, the agent thrust her right hand into the air, made a circular motion, and said curtly, "They're all around here." A number of other passengers who had missed their connecting flights sat up all night in the Atlanta airport, tired and fearful of being mugged.

This scenario is played out daily all across the United States and beyond. "Airline service" is virtually an oxymoron, or contradiction in terms, these days. This industry stands as a highly visible prototype of how not to offer quality. Ask anyone who flies regularly on commercial airlines, and you will almost always elicit a bad experience. How about an airline that ticketed three people for the same seat—and the flight attendant said he couldn't straighten it out because it was time for him to go off duty? When his replacement finally arrived at the seat where the three passengers were waiting, she rudely asked, "What is the problem here?" as though the passengers were somehow at fault.

Selling Hope, Not Cosmetics

As many people see it, marketing is synonymous with advertising, personal selling, or both. Try asking the proverbial man or woman on the street for a definition of the word *marketing*. On the one hand, the word conjures up an image of slick psychologically oriented Madison Avenue media campaigns that attempt, consciously or subliminally, to manipulate people and companies into purchasing things they may not even need or want. As cosmetic executives are supposed to believe, "Women buy hope, not cosmetics." On the other hand, marketing is frequently seen as mostly personal selling and sometimes no more than raw hucksterism.

These stereotypes, born from novels and films, are erroneous. Willy Loman, the sad character in Arthur Miller's play *Death of a Salesman,* really is dead, except in a few industries where abuses in selling are a way of life. Some kinds of door-to-door selling, land dealings in vacation spots, and used car finagling are full of deceitful and fraudulent practices. But in today's global competition with intense media scrutiny, no company can compete very long selling shoddy products on hype. Today's more educated and demanding consumers want to know "Where's the beef?" as the classic advertisement for Wendy's hamburgers asked.

This is not to say that people do not buy products partly on the basis of psychological appeals—of course they do. In his best-selling book, *What They Don't Teach You at Harvard Business School,* Mark McCormack, founder and head of International Management Group and the person *Sports Illustrated* called the most powerful man in sports, described a dinner he had with Andre Heiniger, the chairman of Rolex. Someone asked Heiniger, "How's the watch industry?" He replied, seriously, "Rolex is not in the watch business. We are in the luxury business." McCormack was able to convince Heiniger to sponsor the electronic scoreboard and timing system at Wimbledon because of the excitement, beauty, and charm of Wimbledon and the tennis played there. This sponsorship did not associate Rolex with the mass watchmakers. In reference to the ambience of Wimbledon, Heiniger said, "This is Rolex."

Rolex is certainly in the luxury business. A person can buy a watch that keeps almost perfect time for a small fraction of the price of a Rolex. So Rolex is selling prestige, luxury, and other intangibles. But it is also selling a fine timepiece. If Rolex watches kept poor time or needed frequent repair, Rolex would not be able to sustain its sales on the basis of intangibles alone. In short, there is plenty of substance underlying the luxury appeal. The same is true for cosmetics. A woman may be drawn to a perfume by the allure of its brand name and by the promise and image suggested by its advertising appeals, but the fragrance had better be to her liking. Otherwise, she may not buy twice.

It is hard to imagine any product with more hype than professional wrestling. This form of entertainment is widely ridiculed, but nevertheless it has become so popular that one card drew over ninety thousand people to the Silverdome in Pontiac, Michigan. For the first time in some thirty years, wrestling has reappeared on television during evening prime time. The World Wrestling Federation's Andre the Giant, a seven-foot-five-inch, 520-pound wrestler and the villain to the hero Hulk Hogan, was a guest on CBS's *This Morning* program. Most people who like professional wrestling know that the matches are orchestrated beforehand and the winners predetermined. Is this not proof that hype is more important than substance? No. The people who like professional wrestling would not keep coming back for more if the show were poor. The World Wrestling Federation is the most successful of several competing organizations because its wrestlers and its shows are more entertaining to professional wrestling's devotees. Even in professional wrestling, where hype is pervasive, quality matters to the customers.

Muhammad Ali drew crowds to see his boxing matches partly by being outrageous. He patterned his "I am the greatest" act around his boyhood impressions of a professional television wrestler who went by the name of Gorgeous George. Ali and I grew up in the same years in Louisville, Kentucky. (He was then known as Cassius Marcellus Clay.) He was trained by a Louisville policeman, Joe Martin, whom the twelve-year-old Clay met when he was looking for his stolen bicycle. He fought regularly on a television show on WAVE hosted by the late Ed Kallay, prophetically called *Tomorrow's Champions*. (Future heavyweight champion Jimmy Ellis also appeared on that program.)

I had a chance encounter with then-Cassius Clay in 1963, after a closed-circuit telecast of a world heavyweight championship fight. In that fight, the reigning champion, Charles "Sonny" Liston, demolished former champion Floyd Patterson in the first round, for the second straight fight in less than a year's time. As the crowd left the closed-circuit telecast at the Freedom Hall arena, I saw Clay and asked him how he would fight Liston. His eyes flashed as he came toward me; he punched his right first into the palm of his left hand several times. He screamed for all to hear of what he would do to Liston when they fought the following year, of how he would outmaneuver Liston, wear him down, and eventually administer the coup de grace. Clay was a former Olympic light-heavyweight champion and an undefeated young professional, but Liston was considered by many expert observers to be virtually unbeatable, a fearsome and menacing gladiator steeled by his earlier life in the streets and later in prison, where he had served time for armed robbery. In prison, with the encouragement of the chaplain, Liston had taken up boxing.

Although I admired Clay's ring skills, I wondered if this was not mostly braggadocio he was spouting, at least as far as his chances for beating Liston were concerned. Was he really this confident, or was he just trying to convince himself, or promote ticket sales, or what?

At the weigh-in for the Clay-Liston match in Miami Beach in February 1964, he created such a scene that the fight commission doctor, Alexander Robbins, remarked, "Clay's acting like a man scared to death. He is emotionally unbalanced, liable to crack up before he enters the ring." Dr. Robbins's skepticism was shared by many people—bettors made Clay a 7-1 underdog at fight time.

Was Clay really scared, or was he just feigning it and thereby lulling Liston into complacency? Was he only hyping the fight? Would people pay to see the brash Cassius Clay get his comeuppance? When Liston did not answer the bell for the seventh round against an in-control Clay on the night of February 25, the answer was clear.

Ali was a consummate performer at playing to people's emotions and turning them to his advantage, but he backed up his assertions with deeds. Those who loved him came to see him win, and those who hated him paid their money in hopes he would lose. Others just came to see him "float like a butterfly and sting like a bee," as Ali cornerman and ghetto poet Bundini Brown said. But behind all the psychology, as with Rolex, was substance—greatness. By the time Ali reached middle age, he admitted to shyness, to feeling pressured when surrounded by people, to not feeling great. But, in the face of considerable physical problems of his own, he turned his attention and efforts to helping others, particularly the less fortunate.

Michelin tires are widely considered of superior quality. Michelin, a privately held French-based company, has been very successful in selling tires in the United States by running an ad depicting a baby in diapers sitting inside a Michelin tire. The voice-over makes sure that the viewer gets the idea—buy Michelin for keeping your loved ones safe—by intoning, "Michelin . . . because so much is riding on your tires." Michelin's advertising people have found an effective psychological way to connote quality. Yes, babies do sell tires, as long as the quality of the tires is substantive.

A marketer like Michelin sells steak *and* sizzle, instead of steak *or* sizzle. Strong psychological appeals to people's needs and wants, accompanied by intrinsic product quality, are a blueprint for effective marketing. Steak without at least some sizzle will usually not attract customers, even in business-to-business marketing. But sizzle without steak is a sure recipe for failure.

Quality and Advertising Claims

Emphasis on sizzle at the expense of quality considerations has put a host of American companies in deep trouble, particularly vis-à-vis the Japanese. Nowhere has this been more apparent than in the automobile industry. Until the late 1980s, when American manufacturers began to improve, survey after survey showed that Americans perceived Japanese cars to be durable, reliable, and economical, while they saw American cars as strong on shake, rattle, and roll. As Japanese automobile manufacturers sold quality, value, and economy during the 1970s and 1980s, their U.S. counterparts were heavily promoting exotic appeals based on psychographic or lifestyle approaches to the consumer, a là Farrah Fawcett and the Mercury Cougar.

All segments of consumers are alike in one important way. Regardless of varying lifestyles or whether one is a doctor, lawyer, production-line employee, or you name it, the consumer wants one thing—products that work and services that serve!

A company can build a whole corporate strategy around quality. The issue of quality can be a common goal and a bond among all corporate functions—from production to sales and everything that supports them. For this reason, quality needs to be the daily concern of all employees, from the CEO to the newest hire in maintenance. This achievement is easier said than done, of course, and requires careful employee selection, continual employee training, and a facilitating corporate culture. Union-management relations in one prominent airline became so strained at one point that some of the employees decided to get even with management by doing a poor job. No amount of training could rectify this kind of distrust.

Never advertise product quality if it is not there. Puffery and exaggeration are sure to come back to haunt the company that makes claims that its products and services cannot live up to. From a marketing standpoint, there is nothing worse than unconfirmed customer expectations.

The automobile industry is a highly visible example of a war of words involving quality. Chrysler says that "overall product quality and dealer service" demonstrate that Chrysler has the "highest customer satisfaction of any American car company." Chrysler and the United Auto Workers formed a joint international union-management product quality improvement committee (PQI) in 1980 and in subsequent years ran full-page newspaper ads to celebrate PQI anniversaries. General Motors joins the fray with assertions like "New car owners put three General Motors makes at the top of the list of best-built American cars." Ford counters with quality salvos of its own—that it has "designed and built" the highest-quality American cars and trucks. Various surveys of car owners by independent organizations like J.D. Power, Maritz Market Research, and *Consumer Reports* magazine, all using slightly different criteria, are marshaled to support these quality claims.

Yet Taurus, the most prominent symbol of the quality revival at Ford in the mid-to-late 1980s, was dropped by the *Consumer Reports* "recommended" list in 1988 because of electrical and fuel system problems with the 1986 model. So these quality ratings can be a two-edged sword—a public-relations boost when they recommend favorably, but a PR problem when they recommend negatively. When a company incorporates a favorable product recommendation by an independent rating firm into its advertising claims, it is hard for the company to turn around later and downplay a negative recommendation from the same firm.

Although the quality push by American car companies is a welcome relief from their former "sizzling" advertising strategies based heavily on psychological appeals to customers, there is still too much sizzle. The ads do not say that Japanese cars still generally outperform American cars in quality surveys, regardless of whether they are built in Japan and exported to the United States or assembled in California, Ohio, or Tennessee for domestic sale. The Japanese companies assembling automobiles in the United States —Honda, Nissan, and New United Motor Manufacturing (the Toyota-GM joint venture)—all outperform Ford in quality surveys of car owners, How could Ford make its claim? Simple. Ford says it has "designed and built" the best-quality cars and trucks in the United States—which is technically true: The Japanese cars are *built* in the United States but *designed* in Japan.

I have a better suggestion for automakers than relying on verbal nuances. Why not build cars that beat the Japanese automobiles in customer satisfaction polls and "things gone wrong" surveys, and then advertise superior quality without having to resort to verbal sleight of hand? Shoichiro Irimajiri, president of Honda of America, cogently makes the case for quality: "No matter what a company says. No matter how advanced the technology. The product expresses everything about a company's philosophy, attitude, and commitment."

David Ogilvy, founder of the Ogilvy & Mather advertising agency, is the dean of the advertising fraternity. Some of his advertisements and advertising campaigns are classics—for Hathaway shirts, Rolls-Royce, and Schweppes. Now semiretired, Ogilvy is critical of much of the advertising he sees today. He says there is too much emphasis on "flash" through humor and special effects and not enough on creating advertisements capable of selling. Ogilvy observes that it becomes fashionable every ten to fifteen years in the advertising industry to create messages that entertain. This slant misplaces emphasis on the entertainment value of the messages themselves rather than on whether they can sell.

Marketing and marketers cannot work miracles. Well-designed marketing strategies executed by the best marketing pros cannot compensate for products and services short on performance.

What Is Quality?

Ask three people this question, and you are likely to get three different answers, or maybe no answer at all. Some people take the view, "I cannot define it precisely, but I know it when I see it." Quality can be looked at from the standpoint of technical product quality or as something broader than that. From a marketing strategy perspective, it had better be the broader view.

GenRad is a company that designs, manufactures, and sells test and measurement products to the electronics industry. It says in its annual report that its business is "Automating Quality Management." Its instruments are used in quality control by manufacturers of such products as computers, telecommunications, and office equipment. The firm has become a *Fortune* 500 company by catering to the quality needs of other businesses. Even though GenRad is a highly technical company, heavily staffed with engineers and R&D people, it has found that a commercially workable quality definition must include the consumer.

A company may have the highest-quality product in the world, as measured by laboratory criteria, but it will be for naught if the prospective customer does not see it that way or if the product does not meet the customer's needs as well as a competitive product does. GenRad, this high-tech firm, might be expected to attach a technologically esoteric meaning to the word *quality*. But it says simply yet boldly in its annual report that "Quality products are those which meet customers' expectations. Quality products do what the customers want them to do, at a price they're willing to pay." GenRad means it—its definition is not a public-relations release for public consumption. If you ask GenRad executives in person, they will tell you that quality measurements must include customer perceptions. And perceptions about quality are formed on what the customer thinks about such things as the company's reliability in delivering the goods on time, whether it willingly fulfills what it promises in its warranties, and if it promptly answers inquiries. An unkempt sales rep can send out signals that the company does shoddy work.

GenRad's definition of *quality* is realistic in that it encompasses both customer expectations and price. If a company considers quality in isolation, without regard for customer expectations or for the price he or she is willing to pay, it is flirting with disaster in the marketplace. Think about a woman who usually trades in her car at 50,000 miles. At an odometer reading of 35,000 miles, her car needs new tires. Does she buy a tire with a 45,000-mile life expectancy at $70 per tire, or does she opt for a tire with a 20,000-mile expected wear at $32 a tire? Based on tangibles, the mileage warranty on each tire, she would pay the $70 for the longer-life tire—it is clearly a higher-quality tire. But based on value—the customer's needs and expectations concerning tire life versus price—she would buy the $32 tire.

We normally think of quality problems coming from too little of it. However, it is not at all unusual for a company to build a product or to offer a service that is overkill. The offering is of such high intrinsic quality that it demands a price above what the customer can or is willing to pay. So although most quality problems arise from too little, we can also have too much. Plenty of companies put all the bells and whistles on their offerings only to find out that the customer did not want them. I was once involved in a focus group (in-depth discussion) with a number of engineers who were in charge of purchasing a particular instrument for their employers. Their criticism of one manufacturer's product was that it was too sophisticated for the job it was needed to do. These engineers thought the manufacturer had the highest-quality product of its kind, no doubt about it, but they were unwilling to pay the price when they could get a competitor's version for considerably less.

A company's quality strategy is likely to be the most important competitive decision it makes because this strategy determines how closely customers will perceive the company's offerings as coinciding with their own needs and preferences. Does the company intend to manufacture the absolute highest-quality product in its industry, like 3M? Or does it want to offer the highest-quality product within a certain price range—say, within the compact car market? Maybe the company wants to offer the highest-quality product within all price ranges, perhaps to have an entry in the regular, premium, and imported beer lines. What implications these choices hold! For instance, if the company wants to compete within all price ranges, does it do so with one brand name, like Nike in sport and leisure shoes, or with multiple brand names, like General Electric and Hotpoint in major appliances? The strategy of using several brands implies higher marketing costs, while the strategy of offering one brand across all price ranges risks image problems with the top-of-the-line offerings.

Implementation of strategy is usually just as important as strategy formulation. Yet ironically, it is nonmanagerial personnel—often some of the lowest-paid people in a company—who most determine the quality image conveyed by the company. As far as the customer is concerned, the retail sales clerk, the manufacturer's rep, the flight attendant, or the telephone receptionist *is* the company. A manufacturer may offer the finest product of its kind, technically speaking, but this quality will be eviscerated by a rude sales clerk who, in effect, tells the customer to "take it or leave it" or by a technician who installs the product incorrectly. The same company that spends millions on R&D and advertising may spend, by comparison, a pittance on training its front-line representatives on how to meet the customer. A poorly trained telephone receptionist alone can do untold damage to a company's quality image among its customers—or, more than likely, former customers.

A sign posted near one small-town retailer's cash register typifies the fundamental people-oriented marketing philosophy that is responsible for the prosperity enjoyed by so many companies.

Why Customers Quit

1 Percent	Die
3 Percent	Move Away
5 Percent	Other Friendships
9 Percent	Competitive Reasons
14 Percent	Product Dissatisfaction
68 Percent	Indifference Toward Customer by Some Employee or Employees

Does Quality Pay?

It certainly does. Since 1972, the Profit Impact of Market Strategy (PIMS) program at the Strategic Planning Institute in Cambridge, Massachusetts, has collected and analyzed information contributed by 450 major companies. These companies are large and small, North American and European, public and privately owned; they represent many different types of products and markets, such as high technology, consumer products, services, raw materials, and heavy industrial goods. PIMS is the most extensive and detailed source of information in the world on the question of what kinds of corporate strategic and operational decisions lead to superior profitability.

PIMS has found that no matter what the measure of profitability, be it return on sales or return on investment, profitability is strongly associated with product or service quality *as perceived by customers*. Companies offering products and services that are perceived by customers to be of superior quality, relative to the competition, garner customer loyalty, repeat business, more control over price, market share gains, and lower costs of marketing.

PIMS determines whether a company has a high, medium, or low market share by looking at the company's share relative to its three largest competitors. Consider companies with relatively high market shares and also relatively high perceived product or service quality. They have an average return on investment (ROI) of 38 percent, compared with 20 percent for companies with high market share and low perceived product quality. For medium-market-share companies, the average ROI is 27 percent for companies with products and services perceived to be best and 13 percent for firms with products and services perceived to be inferior. The ROI figures for low-share companies are 21 percent for superior quality and 7 percent for low quality.

PIMS has found that not only does high perceived quality allow a company to have greater control over price, it also has little effect on costs. So companies with high perceived product quality can charge higher prices to customers and achieve costs comparable to competitors. The cliché that "quality is free" is an understatement. Quality pays!

A U.S. Comeback in Quality?

Hardly a week goes by that someone—a congressional representative, a business executive, a writer for a major periodical, a management guru—does not lament the deterioration in quality of American products and services and what it means for the nation's global competitiveness. Tom Peters asks if this is the year when

American business finally gets serious about quality. *Time* runs a feature on the decline of service in the United States. And others voice justifiable concerns about productivity gains, savings levels, deficits, and R&D spending—all issues that, directly or indirectly, impinge on quality.

Still, there is also good news and enough reason for cautious optimism. American companies are responding. For instance, *Fortune* ran a cover story titled "What America Makes Best." The theme of the story is that many U.S. corporations take the quality issue seriously, and this concern has turned them into the world's best competitors in their industries. *Fortune* listed the one hundred products that the United States makes best, from all-electric plastics injection-molding machinery, by Cincinnati Milacron, to washing machines by Maytag and Whirlpool.

Pierre Rinfret says that line-type executives, people from sales and manufacturing, are increasingly influencing American companies today, which he sees as a bright omen. More and more, the people who have been on the corporate firing line, those actually involved in the making and selling of goods and services, those with first-hand experience at manufacturing a car or listening to flesh-and-blood customers, are replacing the staff executives in the upper echelons of companies.

Not long ago, the attitude in many companies was that you put the "dumb" people in manufacturing, especially, and also to a certain extent in sales. The "brighter" folks were to become financial executives, econometricians, attorneys, and strategic planners. A corporate recruiter visiting a prestigious business school to interview someone to work in manufacturing or sales was like the Maytag repairman—the loneliest person in town.

But things are changing, and none too soon. Companies have finally realized that the people who are best able to formulate and implement strategies and tactics for building and selling products that will be competitive in the world marketplace are the people who know production problems and customer concerns best. But there is a long way to go. Look at most MBA programs, and you will see a glaring lack of coursework on production and sales, the core skills in satisfying customers. The law schools continue to pump out record numbers of graduates, which can only lead to an even more litigious society and increased product liability suits and costs of doing business. The Japanese turn out engineers who design and develop products, while we in the United States turn out more lawyers who design and develop additional litigation. On balance, however, great strides have been made by U.S. companies in producing and selling higher-quality offerings.

A Never-Ending Quest

The destination of 100 percent quality is one that companies never reach. There will always be the defective product, the employee who is rude to a customer, or the shipment that arrives late. The best way for a company to know how far it has progressed on its journey toward 100 percent quality is to track customer satisfaction over time. BMW of North America and Rank Xerox Ltd. of Europe tie executive compensation directly to customer satisfaction, as determined by such measures as surveys of customer attitudes and internal audits of repeat sales.

What I call the Consumer's Value Equation is a useful way for a company to assess its competitive position:

Perceived Value
=
The prospective buyer's comparison
of price versus perceived quality

In which quadrant in figure 3–1 would potential and actual customers put your product or service? Where, for example, would Marriott Hotels be placed? Where Motel 6? What about Budweiser, as opposed to all its competitors in the United Kingdom where the brand has not caught on? John Deere versus Caterpillar? If you have more than one product or service or brand, are they positioned in relation to one another and to the competition as you want them to be? If you are an entrepreneur, in which quadrant do you intend to compete? Is this realistic? Will your price/quality combination sell?

Do you know for sure that customers feel this way, or are you mainly guessing? Some executives or entrepreneurs think one thing,

Figure 3–1. *Prospective Buyer's Comparison of Price versus Perceived Quality*

customers another. Perception is usually more important than reality. What the potential buyer thinks is what counts, not whether he or she is right or wrong.

Is the quadrant you are in where you want to be? Does your price/quality strategy appeal to the kinds of customers you have targeted? If so, fine. If not, what needs to be done? Do you have a technically superior product that is not perceived as such? If so, you have a marketing problem. Or do you have a technically inferior product that needs to be upgraded before it is aggressively marketed?

Questions To Ask Youself

1. In addition to the strategic and tactical issues of price versus quality, there is a broader philosophical question that companies need to address: Is management quality-oriented, or is it just paying lip service to the concept? Are employees—from management to the switchboard operators—being regularly trained and monitored on the quality they are providing? Go to Walt Disney World in Orlando, Florida and see how many unhelpful, rude, or sloppy employees you can find. Maybe none. Look over the grounds—see how well-kept and neat they are. Then repeat the test at a non-Disney amusement park. In most cases, the difference

will be noticeable. Disney's unrelenting commitment to quality is why.

2. Is your company spending enough on R&D and automation, or is it scrimping in the interests of short-term return? In attempting to operate efficiently, as a "lean and mean" competitor, has management gone too far in cutting corporate fat and destroyed some of the muscle it will need to compete in the future?

3. Does your market strategy reflect the right mix of steak and sizzle? Do you have a superior product or service that potential customers do not perceive as such because your marketing program is bland? It has been said of more than one boring politician that, if he or she were to give a fireside talk, the fire would go out. Is your marketing program of this ilk? Do you have an exciting and bold marketing program, but a product or service that cannot deliver what is promised? Are you selling too much sizzle and not enough steak?

4
Blunder #3:
Oversubscribing to the
Conventional Wisdom

Progress does not follow a straight line; the future is not a mere projection of trends in the present. Rather, it is revolutionary. It overturns the conventional wisdom of the present, which often conceals or ignores the clues to the future.
—Dr. An Wang, Wang Laboratories

Albert Einstein believed that "imagination is more important than knowledge." He did not say that knowledge is unimportant, only that it is not as important as imagination. Building upon existing knowledge is the way step-by-step progress is made, but bold imagination is the stuff of which progress comes in leaps and bounds.

Another term for society's prevailing knowledge is *conventional wisdom*. Indeed, wisdom means an understanding of what is true, right, or lasting. It equates with common sense or judgment.

Much of the time, the conventional wisdom proves to be correct. But as An Wang, the Chinese immigrant to the United States who founded Wang Laboratories, remarks, the conventional wisdom of the day can also "conceal or ignore the clues to the future." By going against the grain, looking at things from a different vantage point, and discerning or imagining trends that others do not see emerging, a few people in various fields of endeavor act on their perceptions and ride the winds of change to fame and sometimes to fortune. These names go down in the annals of history—the great scientists, inventors, and founders of entire industries.

But most entrepreneurial success stories do not result from revolutionary change, and compared with a Henry Ford, even the most successful of them remain obscure in the scheme of history. In most cases, the entrepreneur sees a better way to do a job or meet an unfulfilled need and innovates accordingly. Later, people typically say, "That was so simple—why didn't I think of it?" The answer itself is simple: Because, as with the innovators of revolutionary change, the entrepreneur was not bound by the conventional wisdom, whereas most people were. His or her imagination transcended the knowledge of the day about something as mundane as designing a wrench, cooking a chicken dinner, or selling soap.

Innovative and creative marketers eye the conventional wisdom with healthy skepticism. They look for opportunities that the pack does not see. Majority opinion, or a strong consensus, is not infallible by any means, and statistics are subject to various interpretations. Suppose these individuals had listened to what many "experts" said: Christopher Columbus—"the world is flat"; Wright Brothers— "if man were meant to fly, he would have been born with wings"; and Ronald Reagan—"too old to run for president—he can't win."

Misjudgments of the Conventional Wisdom

Thomas Malthus proposed in the nineteenth century that population tends to increase more rapidly than the food supply. Unless it is voluntarily controlled through lower birthrates or by war, disease, or famine, poverty is inevitable. This Malthusian proposition has been passed down through textbooks and embraced by numerous groups and people. But Thomas Sowell, a senior fellow at the Hoover Institution, has pointed out that the world's food supply has been growing consistently faster than the world's population, and that there are vast amounts of unused fertile land. Moreover, the entire population of the planet Earth could be housed in one-story, single-family houses in Texas at a population density less than that of some cities in the United States.

College students of the 1950s and 1960s were often advised to get a teaching certificate because if need be, they could "always teach." Not long thereafter, teaching jobs were hard to come by. Somebody forgot to consider that the post–World War II baby boom might not go on forever. State governors and legislators were so caught up in the population explosion of college-age citizens in the 1960s that they built and expanded colleges and universities as if the U.S. would soon outgrow the People's Republic of China. The Soviet Union's launch of Sputnik in 1957 created a rush to engineering schools and to physics departments. In the 1960s and early 1970s, the market for aerospace engineers ran out of steam, and physics doctorates could be found selling shoes.

Students of today are counseled to go into computer-related occupations. This conventional advice almost guarantees a coming job glut. It is reminiscent of the poolside party scene in the movie *The Graduate*, at which the recent college graduate, played by Dustin Hoffman, asks the business tycoon what he, the graduate, should do with his life. The tycoon, ever so confidently, advises him to seek a career in plastics.

An Achilles' heel of conventional wisdom can be found in any line of endeavor or in any school of thought. For years, physicians subscribed to the belief that patients frequently wake up from surgery shivering because they are cold as a result of being only partially covered, of receiving cold intravenous fluids, and of having cold air pumped into their lungs. This belief has now been discredited. The shivering results from the process whereby the anesthetics used to render patients unconscious wear off at different rates in the spine and brain. The spinal cord comes back from anesthesia faster than the brain, which means that the spine is chemically disconnected from the brain. This chemical separation leads to abnormal reflexes or tremors resembling shivering.

Misjudging Human Potential and Horsepower

The very best knowledge that society or a field of endeavor has does not guarantee that it can pick winners and losers. These geniuses—Sir Isaac Newton, Thomas Alva Edison, and Albert Einstein—were all badly misjudged early in their lives. The conventional wisdom of those who knew them early in life was that they were unremarkable.

Isaac Newton was born in 1643, but his intellectual talents did not become obvious until he was in his twenties. In 1665,

Newton was forced to return home to Lincolnshire, England, from Trinity College, where he was a student; Trinity had been closed by the plague. In the next eighteen months, his talents blossomed; he initiated great advances in astronomy, mathematics, physics, and optics. Newton's *Principia* may stand as the premier work of science. Early in Newton's life, his own mother apparently failed to recognize her son's potential. She took him out of grammar school for what proved to be a failed effort to train him to manage her estate.

Thomas Edison, no doubt the greatest inventor of all time, had only three months of formal schooling. He did not adjust to the routine of school and was thought by his teacher to be confused and intellectually slow. The teacher called him "addled" or mixed up. Edison's mother tutored him at home. His early work years were spent as a telegraph operator, a period of time when he developed an urge to be an inventor.

Albert Einstein also had problems in school and a disdain for formal instruction. Although he remained in school, his uncle tutored him in mathematics at home. Einstein was admitted to the Federal Polytechnic in Zurich, Switzerland, on his second attempt—he flunked the entrance exam the first time around. After graduation, he had a hard time obtaining a job, but finally landed a position with the Swiss patent office. Three years later he published his first paper on relativity, which he had completed while working full time at his patent-office job.

Proponents of the wisdom of the day in the time of Galileo Galilei caused the father of experimental physics and modern mechanics to spend the last eight years of his life under house arrest near Florence, Italy. Galileo's perfection of the newly invented telescope had enabled him to make the astronomical observations needed to confirm the Copernican theory that the sun is the center of the solar system and the planets revolve around it. This achievement, and Galileo's contention that mathematics— rather than Aristotle's verbal method—was the correct way to study nature, put him squarely at odds with the powerful Aristotelian professors in the universities and with the Catholic Church. Copernican theory and Scripture were contradictory, which riled the Jesuits. At the Inquisition in Rome in 1633, Galileo's conclusions, particularly in the book *Dialogue of the Two Chief World Systems*, were found to be heresy. After perfunctorily recanting his previous errors, Galileo was permanently exiled to his home.

The story of Galileo is not unusual. Descartes conceived of gravitation, but himself considered it to be occult. Charles Darwin and his theory of evolution were widely considered to be evil in his day, and still are in some quarters. Sigmund Freud was ridiculed and hated by many for his revolutionary psychoanalytic theories.

Every year, sports fans of professional football and basketball teams anxiously await the draft of college players. Hope springs eternal. A few years later, some of the star college players who were high draft choices are no longer in the professional ranks or are bench warmers, while a few of the unknowns, often from obscure colleges, who were not highly regarded coming out of college, are excelling. Johnny Unitas, one of the best professional football quarterbacks of all time, was playing for a semiprofessional team when the Baltimore Colts signed him as a free agent.

Annually in July, sheikhs, wealthy English bookmakers, industrialists, corporate raiders, renowned breeders, prominent hardboots, and other high rollers converge on Lexington, Kentucky, to buy and sell yearling Thoroughbred racehorse prospects at the Keeneland summer sales. The July auctions at Keeneland are the crème de la crème. Only the yearlings with the bluest of bloodlines and the best of conformation are allowed in. Conventional wisdom says, "Breed the best to the best, and expect the best." The trouble is, however, that the conventional wisdom is not always right. Many of the bluebloods in the July sale prove to be slow of foot or injury-prone, and a few of their less fashionable relatives become winners. Canonero II brought $1,200 at the 1969 Keeneland September sale of yearlings (a fall sale for animals with a pedigree and/or conformation not up to the standards required of summer-sale yearlings). Canonero II had mediocre ancestors and a crooked right foreleg. After he was initially campaigned in Puerto Rico against second-rate competition, Canonero II was sent to the United States in 1971 and trained by unorthodox methods by a little-known trainer. He won the Kentucky Derby and the Preakness Stakes. He was so lightly regarded in the Derby that the track handicapper had relegated him to the mutuel field. The mutuel field is a single grouping, for betting purposes, that the track handicapper uses as a catchall for several horses thought to have little chance to win.

Misjudging Concepts and Innovations

Look in the telephone book yellow pages of any city with a population of more than 100,000, under the restaurant listings. Contemplate the wide variety of choices. Now try to think of a business opportunity for a new or modified restaurant theme. It would be difficult for most people to envision a new fast-food concept that would have nationwide or international franchise potential. Restaurants already offer almost any menu imaginable; what opportunity for something new is there? Yet Chi-Chi's Mexican restaurant chain became a magnificent winner in only a very few years. But back when Chi-Chi's was nothing but a concept, probably only a small percentage of people would have invested their money on the gamble that Americans would support a full-service Mexican restaurant chain.

When John Y. Brown bought control of Kentucky Fried Chicken from Harland Sanders, fast-food franchising was not a crowded field. But many of the conventional thinkers told Brown that he could not sell southern fried chicken through franchise outlets in the North. People living north of the Mason-Dixon line supposedly had no taste for the product.

Federal Express was the pioneering company in the overnight delivery of business packages. In 1979, it had revenues of $160.3 million and 5,600 employees. By 1987, the company was moving 900,000 packages every business day through Memphis, Tennessee. It was doing $3.2 billion in sales—about half the industry revenues—and employed 41,000 people. Federal Express's founder, former pilot Frederick Smith, had once received a grade of C in college on a term paper that proposed his idea for an overnight delivery service. The professor had evidently thought the idea impractical.

In the years immediately following World War II and well into the late 1950s, the prevailing wisdom in Japan was that Japan did not need to develop a strong automobile manufacturing capability.

The country could rely on the American car companies. Shoichiro Honda was pressured by the Japanese government-business establishment to concentrate his efforts on motorcycles. So it was in the face of strong and united opposition that Honda built his automobile business. It would have been almost unimaginable then that the Japanese automobile companies, and especially Honda, would be the world presence they are today.

Avoiding Sweeping Generalizations

Marketers hear and talk all the time about the aging of society and what it means for selling goods and services. The "gray" market of people fifty-five years of age and over is certainly a reality. This segment of the population in the United States comprises over 30 percent of all adults, and their numbers are growing at double the rate of the overall population.

The gray market is usually discussed as if it were homogenous with regard to buyer behavior and purchasing power, which is erroneous. There are significant differences. In the late 1980s, almost one-half the mature market is comprised of people 55–64; about one-third is accounted for by the 65–74 age bracket; and slightly over 20 percent is in the 75 and older grouping. However, in the years ahead, the 75-and-older category will grow rapidly, eventually reaching 29 percent of the 55 and over population, while the 65–74 group will increase by only 5 percent and the 55–64 category will decline. The younger segment, 55–64, will not grow again until the first of the post–World War II baby-boom generation reaches 55 in 2001.

These three age segments of the gray market have different consumption patterns. Individuals 55 years old are just as close to 35 as they are to 75. Some of their purchasing patterns resemble the former, some the latter. The 55–64 age group spends more than the average U.S. family, whereas the 65–74 age bracket spends less than average, and the 75 and older population spends the least of any age segment. But even these figures mask important consumption differences. The 55–64-year-olds spend heavily on apparel, food, pension programs, and insurance but lightly on housing and education. Citizens in the 65–74 age category spend more than average on newspapers and health care but less on apparel and food. They also have the most purchasing power of any age segment of society. More than half of them have income that is double the poverty level. The 75 and over population spends far below average on everything except health care, on which they spend the most. The gray market is relatively affluent. Only one-sixth of people living in poverty are over 55, which is counter to the popular stereotype. Since 1980, the income of 65-and-over households has risen three times faster than all American households.

In the mid-to-late 1980s, the Hispanic population in the United States is nearly 19 million—a 30 percent increase since 1980. Fifty-four percent of these live in California and Texas. Many companies have reacted to the Hispanic market with special marketing efforts. For instance, as might be expected, most advertising money is spent in Los Angeles, Miami, New York, Chicago, San Francisco, and a few other cities. But marketers have found that, just as there is no gray market in the singular, there is also no one Hispanic market. Rather, there are several Hispanic markets. Most Hispanics prefer to converse in Spanish, but many younger and more affluent Hispanics like English better. It cannot be assumed that advertisements that appeal to Caribbean Hispanics will be liked by Mexican-Americans. Campbell's Soup has used three different advertising campaigns to market to Hispanics—one for Caribbean Hispanics, one for Mexican-Americans, and another that combines elements of the other two.

Blacks are another important population segment that is often categorized too quickly. In some things, blacks do tend to act in unison, such as in voting for Democratic Party candidates in national and local elections. But for many products and services, there is no such homogenous buyer behavior. Instead, as with the Caucasian and Hispanic populations, there are segments in the black population that can be identified along demographic and social-class lines, and these segments exhibit differences in buying behavior from one another.

Looking Beyond the Aggregate Statistics

Marketers who look superficially at the statistics propagated by various government agencies run the risk of glossing over meaningful information buried in the data or of drawing the wrong conclusions. The same can be said for interpreting and analyzing the results of studies by private-sector organizations. The seemingly obvious can be deceiving.

Marketers need to do their own probing of statistics and their own deep thinking about what they mean and augur for industries, markets, and companies. Economic reports in the electronic media in particular, where there is little time for in-depth analysis, often convey misleading conclusions from government and private-sector reports.

According to a study by Find/SVP, a New York City market research firm, as of the late 1980s approximately 13.5 percent of all U.S. households earn more than $50,000 annually. So companies that want to market to affluent customers should focus their efforts on these 28.5 million people, right? Wrong. The Find/SVP study revealed that about 3.5 million households with net worths of more than $250,000 have incomes of less than $50,000 a year. These 3.5 million households would not be categorized as affluent by the $50,000 annual-income affluence criterion, but they surely would constitute a prime market for upscale goods and services. The study also reported that 20 percent of families who earn $50,000 to $75,000 annually have a head of household who is a woman or a black—and this percentage is likely to increase to 33 percent within two to three years. Forty percent of the heads of households in the lower end of the $50,000-to-$75,000 annual-income range are not college graduates; and 20 percent are blue-collar or sales employees. Why, then, do advertising campaigns for upscale products concentrate on reaching Caucasian couples, ages 35 to 54, headed by male professionals and executives who are college graduates?

Perhaps no bit of economic wisdom has been more repeated by politicians, news commentators, and assorted pundits than the purportedly growing rich-versus-poor split in American society. But income concentration in the United States is close to the same now as it was in 1960. Since 1950, the real income of Americans has doubled, and all income classes have consistently shared in this progress in the standard of living. There is also freedom to enhance or lose one's income position in the United

States. A University of Michigan study by Greg Duncan revealed a great deal of family-income mobility, meaning that people are not ensconced or stuck, as the case may be, in a certain income range. Over 50 percent of the children from the top income level move down at least one level from generation to generation, and almost half the children from the bottom income rung move up one level. Only 40 percent of all families remain in the same income level from one generation to the next.

An Associated Press story headlined in newspapers across the United States featured some decidedly pessimistic conclusions. A public policy professor and a Washington, D.C., institute researcher had concluded that the middle class is in trouble and that young Americans will be unable to reach the standard of living achieved by their parents' generation. "What went wrong?" they asked. At the same time, a syndicated Knight-Ridder article blazed headlines that the savings tradition of Americans is dying.

The very same month, a *Forbes* magazine cover story—"Are We a Nation of Spendthrifts?"—gave quite a different picture. Despite variable economic conditions over the past thirty-five years, savings rates have been highly stable. In addition to adducing plenty of backup data—from three measures that track national savings—*Forbes* consulted with several academic and business economists who corroborated what the data indicated.

Ben Wattenberg, in his book *The Good News is the Bad News is Wrong*, cites statistic after statistic, poll after poll, and sign after sign that run counter to what is popularly promulgated (and no doubt widely believed) about the U.S. economy and the American way of life. Take several economic and social issues, for instance. Per capita personal income grew 35 percent between 1972 and 1985 in real dollars. At that kind of growth, our grandchildren would have twice our present income at a much earlier age. The percentage of married couples under 35 who own their own homes was 62 percent in 1980, compared with 38 percent in 1950. The percent of population below the poverty line went from 22.4 percent in 1959 to 8–9 percent in 1984. The elderly in poverty dropped from 35.2 percent in 1959 to 14.1 percent in 1983. Federal spending on social safety-net programs was $155 billion in 1970 and $403 billion in 1985. Minority-group teenagers have the same unemployment rates as adults, when only nonstudents are considered. Concerning the United States' widely lamented slippage in technological leadership: Between 1901 and 44, Americans won 17 percent of the Nobel prizes for science; between 1980 and 83, they won 68 percent. In 1983, all the Nobel science prizes went to U.S. citizens. How about America's rumored deindustrialization? There were 19.4 million American manufacturing jobs in 1970; there were 19.6 million such jobs in 1983. Moreover, this constant-size work force increased its total production by about 36 percent in real terms. Finally, on values: Reputable (Gallup, Yankelovich, and the like) public opinion surveys show Americans to be the most family-centered, religious, and sexually conservative people in the industrialized West.

My intent in citing these examples is not to debunk popular thought or to provoke debate. Rather, it is to show that a savvy marketer does not allow statistics to go unchallenged or routinely accepted at face value. The shrewd marketer plays the role of devil's advocate to satisfy himself that the statistics really mean what they seem to mean.

The prevailing wisdom can be off the mark not only through pessimistic or doomsday interpretations of statistics and gossip— "The federal budget deficit is going to throw us into a worldwide catastrophe that will make the 1930s look like a minor recession." It can also be off target through blithe optimism—"The budget deficit will correct itself, there is no need to worry." Statistics and studies that paint an overly bright picture of the future can obscure emerging trends that represent threats to an industry or business that end up blind siding it. In virtually every industry that has been destroyed by the invention, development, and commercialization of a better technology, the threatened firms ignored or underestimated the technological challenge to their existence. Vacuum-tube manufacturers reacted to the invention of the transistor by pouring more money into R&D—on vacuum tubes. It was during this period of their imminent demise that vacuum tubes reached their highest level of technological performance capability.

Vacuum tubes are gone forever, then—relics of the past? No, this conventional wisdom too is wrong. Vacuum tubes are poised for a comeback. Work done by SRI International in California has made it possible to produce vacuum tubes to microdimensions—smaller than a human hair. And these microtubes can accommodate much more electrical current than silicon-based transistors: electrons move through a vacuum some twenty times faster than through silicon. These microtubes open up all kinds of possibilities in faster communications and supercomputers. After four decades of conventional wisdom that vacuum tubes were obsolete, it appears that some rethinking is in order.

A marketer needs to adopt an objective posture toward statistics and studies, taking a clinical let-the-chips-fall-where-they-may and don't-believe-everything-you-hear attitude. With a factual, in-depth, and questioning approach to the evidence, a company can discern both the opportunities and the threats in the societal environment in which it operates.

Rednecks, Blue and White Collars, Bluebloods, and Country Music

If a company wants to sell to a market segment of people who prefer pickup trucks, stock car racing, or bowling, and work at blue-collar and agricultural jobs, then advertise on the local country-music station. That is the stereotype, which happens to be a partial picture at best and more descriptive of the 1950s than the Space Age.

The Country Music Association commissioned a study (*The Country Music Radio Listener . . . A New Profile*) by the Arbitron rating service that confirmed what many people have long suspected or known. Compared to the overall population of the United States, a larger percentage of country-music listeners are affluent, well-educated professionals. They are more likely than the average American citizen to have access to such upscale financial services as a Visa Gold Card. Forty percent of all country-music listeners are in America's highest socioeconomic groups.

Country-music artists perform at Carnegie Hall and Madison Square Garden. The late patrician Nelson Rockefeller was a fan of Willie Nelson's music and the Yale-educated George Bush listens to the Oak Ridge Boys and Loretta Lynn.

Some connoisseurs of the Metropolitan Opera no doubt believe that its country cousin, the Grand Ole Opry, is on the airwaves only because of some past lapse in FCC standards. But today, many of the people like those who attend the Met in New York tune their radios to stations that play slice-of-life songs with lyrics about lovin', cheatin', drinkin', and raisin' Cain and kids. Astute marketers know that country can be a state of mind as well as a location.

Conventional Wisdom Where?
Parris Island or Paris, France?

Once on an automobile trip to Florida, I stopped for breakfast at a restaurant in rural Georgia. The waitress inquired whether I wanted grits with my bacon and eggs. Making small talk, I asked, "Aren't grits customarily served with breakfast in Georgia?" She said she always asked the customer before serving grits because "certain" people may not know what they are or have an aversion to them. She went on to say that if a customer asks for "a grit" with breakfast, it is a sure sign he or she is a Yankee or other foreigner.

Indeed, there are differences in culture and tastes within most countries, and these are reflected in the way people behave as consumers. Mass communications has had a homogenizing effect, but important differences still remain, some deeply rooted in ethnic traditions.

In the global business environment of the latter part of the twentieth century, provincialism and long-propagated wisdom can lead companies and entrepreneurs to miss the boat completely on emerging opportunities. Who would have thought that that exemplar of the free market system, McDonald's, would be permitted to open restaurants in the Soviet Union? Or that American soft drinks would be sold in the People's Republic of China?

The Soviet Union is beset by the economic stagnation that inevitably occurs whenever individual incentives for productivity are discouraged or prohibited. Mikhail Gorbachev, the Soviet leader, has been searching for a philosophically acceptable way to accommodate a worker-manager incentive system within the framework of Marxist-Leninist theory. His unresolvable problem is simply that the logical evolution of incentives is called *capitalism*. So the Russian theorists have decided to attempt to separate markets from capitalism. In dramatic contrast to Soviet central planning, market forces—customer demand—will to a much larger extent be allowed to determine which goods and services are produced and sold, and in what quantities. But unlike capitalism, land, labor, and capital will continue to be tightly controlled by the central Soviet government. This obviously will not work because there will be an inefficient allocation of resources—land, labor, and capital. Under the Russian concept, a manufacturing plant could be located in the heart of Moscow, since private investors would not be allowed to bid up the price of land and thereby signal that midtown Moscow is too expensive for manufacturing and has more appropriate uses. The point is, however, the lengths to which the Russians are going to maintain their conventional wisdom—communism—while at the same time achieving their anathema—some "bad" old-fashioned free enterprise.

In an apocryphal story, Gorbachev's mother visits her son's dacha for the first time and sees the fine furnishings and the servants, and Raisa Gorbachev's furs and jewels. Startled and concerned for her Mikhail's safety, she asks, "But Mikhail, what will you do if the Communists happen to see this?"

The globalization of business touches almost every business in the industrialized countries. If a business does not sell overseas, it buys overseas, or at least it buys products made with foreign parts. One of the ingredients in the success stories both at Ford Motor and at Chrysler is their outsourcing of parts purchases. Becoming global acquirers of parts and entire cars has enabled them to purchase in the most efficient manner and produce cars less expensively than General Motors, which has continued to do business with its own parts subsidiaries.

Too many smaller businesses continue to operate domestically, as they always have. One might ask, Is not "doing business on an international basis" for the "big boys"? Hardly. Many smaller businesses participate in exporting. State and local agencies help them by providing information, counseling, and encouragement.

One mistake in global marketing is for a business executive to assume that the conventional wisdom in one country is appropriate for another country. Several pages or more could be filled with blunders that companies have committed because they did not bother to check out how a product name would translate into another language, or how advertising copy would be interpreted in another country, or whether the product would be offensive for religious reasons, or whether the nation was on the metric system, or . . . A detergent advertisement by one U.S. firm was a disaster in Middle East nations because it inadvertently conveyed exactly the wrong point. The print ad showed dirty clothes piled on the left, the company's detergent in the center, and clean clothes carefully stacked on the right. To a Middle Easterner, who reads from right to left, the message was that the soap soils the clothes.

Contrarian Thinking

No "yes" men or women need apply—this should be the philosophy of creative marketers. If the wisdom of the day happens to be true, then acting on it can produce results. Anyone who readily affirms the conventional wisdom may turn out to be a good marketing functionary. However, the conventional wisdom can be wrong, and for that reason, it needs to be challenged. Entrepreneurial opportunities may present themselves.

No, a company does not have to hire a guru, an avant-garde, or a mystic. Creative thinkers who can play the role of devil's advocate concerning the conventional wisdom are found in pinstriped business suits as well as in more free-spirited attire. Most outstanding entrepreneurs were once people plugging along at everyday life who had insight and the courage to act on it. Some of the self-made people on the *Forbes* 400 list of wealthiest Americans had unexceptional educational and work histories before they excelled. In fact, some of them were considered mediocre performers and failures.

Many companies that hire college graduates screen them initially on the basis of grade-point average. The students below a certain cutoff are not interviewed. Is this ever a mistake! Some of the most successful entrepreneurs would have been excluded under a grade-point-average criterion. One multimillionaire entrepreneur, reflecting on his life, commented, "I earned F's in school and A's in business." A prominent lawyer who has tried numerous capital offense cases and never lost says that, with his college record, he would not be admitted today to any prestigious law school. By modern standards, Edison and Einstein would be unlikely candidates for admission to a first-level graduate school. Edison would probably have been denied admission to college at all.

Companies tend to hire college graduates who have done well in academic programs stressing analytical skills. In so doing, creative and entrepreneurial individuals are often passed over. The universities, especially some of the business schools, contribute to the problem by overemphasizing analysis and quantification and underemphasizing communications, selling, and entrepreneurship. Fortunately, this orientation is beginning to change, although at a snail's pace.

The Sherlock Holmes Method

The peerless fictional detective Sherlock Holmes would have made a marvelous lecturer on how the conventional wisdom should be approached by entrepreneurs and marketers. The keen skills of observation that Holmes developed enabled him to see signs and hear nuances that others overlooked. As the famous resident of Victorian London's 221B Baker Street advised about examining information for potential clues and evidence, whenever one eliminates the impossible, whatever is left, however improbable, must contain the solution.

A solution, for an entrepreneur or manager, may be a new product, a new business, or even a new industry that is the answer to customer needs and wants. The marketer scans government statistics, looks at surveys and polls, and observes change firsthand as a member of society. As Sherlock Holmes said, the task is one of sorting through this mass of information, eliminating the impossible and irrelevant, and interpreting what the rest means in terms of market opportunities and threats. People and companies basically have access to the same general information, so it is the interpretation of that information—what it means for the future— that determines individual and commercial destiny.

Nor are successful entrepreneurs and marketers of new products too hasty in dismissing unconventional conclusions about emerging societal and industry trends as nonsequiturs (conclusions that do not follow logically from the information at hand). They may end up accepting what the statistics and trends seem to be saying—but not before they apply the kind of looking-beyond-the-obvious and ever-probing approach of a Sherlock Holmes. That is the process by which insight leads to concepts for new products, services, and businesses. And subtleties overshadowed by overall trends can point to opportunities for serving profitable market niches.

Encouraging Devil's Advocacy

The term *devil's advocate* derives from a practice of the Roman Catholic Church in blessing or conferring sainthood on a deceased person. The devil's advocate is the Church official whose duty it is to point out defects in the evidence on which the demand for beatification or canonization rests. The term has been popularized and generally refers to a person who argues for or against a cause to test its validity or for the sake of debate.

Every aspiring entrepreneur and marketer needs to embrace the concept of devil's advocacy. By doing so, two things can result, both of them favorable. First, challenging the conventional wisdom can expose where it is wrong or where there are niches or contrarian "against-the-grain" opportunities in broad societal trends. Second, argumentation can often save time, effort, and capital that would otherwise be expended on a new product, service, or business that has a commercial Achilles' heel.

The Association for Collegiate Entrepreneurs (ACE) is a student organization that is springing up on college campuses. One service that some local ACE chapters provide is the screening of ideas for new business ventures by would-be entrepreneurs from the community. It is amazing how much insight and information someone with an idea, product prototype, or business can get at an ACE meeting full of young and inexperienced college students. The entrepreneur usually goes away with a better handle on what it would take to make a success of the proposed venture or whether it is in fact even commercially viable. At ACE meetings, the critiquers—the students—have no vested interest, and their comments tend to be candid—so much so that the entrepreneur had better have a thick skin.

In organizations, employees tend not to be so candid because of the normal inhibitions. For example, it may be politically risky to criticize a project that is near and dear to the boss. Some of the biggest new-product blunders of all time have occurred because a company stubbornly pursued an obviously lost cause. Ego prevailed over the abort signals that the market research or marketplace was sending. A stifling environment is what management must continually work against. Senior management's role is to create the right corporate climate for a devil's advocacy process to work and then to hire enough contrarian thinkers who are not afraid to express their opinions.

Most corporate employees will not and should not be contrarian thinkers. Some corporate tasks—accounting and computers, for instance—are essentially analytical and routine. But a few creative thinkers are needed for balance. One company experimented with various right brain/left brain combinations of people in problem solving. Right-brain individuals tend to be creative and imaginative, whereas left-brain people are more analytical and mathematically inclined. Some folks, of course, have a mixture of both. This company gave three groups of employees the same problem to work on. One group was comprised of left-brain analytical types, the second was made up of right-brain creative individuals, and the third included some creative people and some who were analytical. The third group took twice as long as the other two groups to solve the problem, but the solution was far superior. The creative/analytical clash had resulted in a great deal of debate, which led to a solution representing a synthesis of creative and analytical thinking.

Questions to Ask Yourself

1. Do you encourage people to challenge the conventional wisdom?

2. Is creative and contrarian thinking promoted?

3. Do you have the right people to do the thinking? Would a young Ross Perot, Fred Smith, or Ted Turner be valued or anathema in your company? General Motors wanted the ever-questioning Perot off its board of directors, so much that it bought

him out. Perot's great sin was that he wanted change, wanted General Motors to build better cars and save their market share. He did little things that irritated the GM brass, like visit Chevrolet dealerships to see how customers were treated. Such heresy!

4. Do you probe government and industry statistics and market research for things that others may not see? Or do you just take them at face value and draw the same conclusions as most people?

5. Do you believe that imagination is just as important as knowledge, or more so, in identifying commercial opportunities? What is being done to encourage it on an ongoing basis?

5

Blunder #4:
Putting Too Much Faith
in Forecasting

Boast not thyself of tomorrow, for thou knowest not what a day may bring forth.

—Proverbs 27:1

C onventional wisdom is usually the basis for prediction, since people generally subscribe to the idea that the best guide to the future is the past. But in a time of rapid change like today, this generalization is less true. Some of mankind's most revolutionary innovations would have been delayed had the innovator listened to the consensus of the time regarding what the future held in store. And some revolutionary innovations no doubt were delayed because the prevailing wisdom dissuaded the innovators.

Commercial opportunities, some of which prove to be earth-shaking in their effects on society but most of which do not, present themselves to entrepreneurs and corporate managers who do not put too much faith in forecasting. Many experts of the day are bound by the existing state of knowledge, and therefore they are myopic in projecting future trends. They lack the imagination that is so important to progress.

The Nostradamus Syndrome

Psychics, soothsayers, clairvoyants, swamis, gurus, seers, sages, fortune-tellers, prophets, astrologers, numerologists, tea leaf readers, horoscope casters, crystal ball peerers, dealers in cards or talismans—forget them all for predicting future events with consistency and certainty. No mortal and no technique sees around corners and peers into the future with regular accuracy. Management philosopher Peter Drucker has said that forecasting is not a respectable human activity. Drucker's skeptical view of forecasting has been shared by people for thousands of years. In Deuteronomy 18:9, the Bible talks about the abomination committed when anyone practices divination or uses soothsaying, augury, sorcery, a charmer, a medium, a wizard, or a necromancer.

Nostradamus, a sixteenth-century French astrologer-philosopher, supposedly prophesied that an earthquake caused by a unique planetary alignment would destroy the "New City" in May 1988. Some Californians took this to mean Los Angeles or possibly San Francisco. During May 1988 in the Golden State, special Nostradamus crisis phone lines for psychological counseling were clogged with panicky people; the Griffith Observatory received dozens of calls; and a few Los Angeles residents left town to avoid the impending earthquake.

When former Reagan White House chief of staff Donald Regan alleged that Nancy Reagan consulted a San Francisco astrologer about her husband's schedule, most people were amused, dismissed it as an attempt to hype book sales, or thought that Regan was trying to extract revenge for his firing as chief of staff. However, a number of people commented that astrology would save Ronald Reagan from the supposed die-in-office jinx that afflicts Presidents who are Aquarians and/or are elected in years ending in a zero— William Henry Harrison, Abraham Lincoln, James Garfield, William McKinley, Franklin Roosevelt, and John Kennedy.

The legitimate methods of forecasting have nothing in common with astrology, numerology, or any of the other scientifically baseless ways to predict the future. But sometimes the legitimate techniques have the same effect—what I call the Nostradamus syndrome—on the people who read them, especially if they are based on thick stacks of computer print-outs or made by a highly reputable individual or organization.

Many of the same business people who scoff at unscientific methods of forecasting readily embrace forecasts based on econometric modeling and expert opinion by individuals and so-called think tanks staffed by demographers, sociologists, engineers, and others. These forecasters are well educated and skilled in methodology, but their track record is not particularly good. Even the leading indicators of economic activity maintained and published by the federal government are no longer as accurate as they once were in foretelling changes in economic activity. They are apt to send off conflicting and erroneous signals.

Economists have long been targets of criticism and jokes; that is nothing new. The decisive President Harry Truman once asked his staff if they would find him a few one-armed economic advisers, so that when the economists presented him with a forecast, they could not hedge by saying "on the other hand." To spoof forecasting, a group calling itself the Procrastinators' Society meets every year on New Year's Eve to make predictions—with great accuracy—for the year that is about to expire at midnight.

The acclaimed public television program *Wall Street Week* annually asks a panel of stock market experts for their predictions for the New York Stock Exchange listings. A year later, the predictions are compared to what actually resulted. Not only are many of the predictions wrong by a large margin, but even the stock pickers who are right have a difficult time sustaining that performance level from year to year. A number of the premier stock brokerage firms in the United States annually recommend portfolios of stocks that do not outperform the Dow-Jones averages.

In the 1980s, the *Harvard Business Review* reprinted some of the forecasts from its 1971 article titled "What Businessmen Expect From the 1970s." Some of the projections, which had been obtained from a survey of executives in prominent companies with access to expert opinion and the best in forecasting techniques, were for an average 4.5 percent inflation rate, a 5.5 percent unemployment rate, and relatively mild recessions. Little could they know of the coming wage-price freeze, the Arab oil embargo, the severe recession, and the 20 percent prime lending rate.

An often-heard adage is that hindsight vision is 20/20. But it is not. Sometimes a person can look back on a key decision in life and still not be sure he or she made the right choice. So if not even hindsight is 20/20, coping with an unknowable future is infinitely more difficult. That is why entrepreneurs and managers who try to get ready for the future by relying heavily on expert forecasts are expecting too much. When a future different from the one they expected materializes, they can pay a stiff price.

Expert Predictions in History

One section of the Henry Ford Museum in Dearborn, Michigan, is devoted to a collection of people's conceptions of the future. Ideas from the 1920s and 1930s about what life would be like toward the end of the twentieth century are expressed by scale models of cities, artists' renderings, and movies. Most of them are far off target. A person viewing these can readily see just how difficult it is to predict fifty or sixty years into the future. In the period of rapid technological change of today, in which a half-century of progress by historical standards may be compressed into a third of a decade, forecasting for only a few years away is hazardous. How many people would have thought in 1975 that personal computers would be as widely used as they are now? Practically no one. And the revolutionary advances in biotechnology would have seemed like science fiction.

An individual's society and its knowledge base provide the constraining frame of reference that makes it hard to comprehend what changes the future will bring. The present is like a mental form of gravity that limits people from jumping too far away from the existing state of knowledge.

I am a collector of expert predictions. As you read some of them, try to put yourself in the position of a person living in the time in which the predictions were made. What would have been your reaction if you had heard the forecasts coming from the experts who made them? If you were a gambler, would you have bet for or against the forecasts? If you were an investor or company president, would you have committed resources to develop and commercialize such products and ventures as anesthesia, the automobile, the airplane, the submarine, television, "talking pictures," and nuclear energy? How about one of the most famous movies of all time, a legendary actress, and the king of rock 'n' roll music?

Expert Predictions About Technology

"What can be more palpably absurd than the prospect held out of locomotives traveling twice as fast as stagecoaches?"
—*The Quarterly Review*, 1825

~~~~~

"The abolishment of pain in surgery is a chimera. It is absurd to go on seeking it today. Knife and pain are two words in surgery that must forever be associated in the consciousness of the patient. To this compulsory combination we shall have to adjust ourselves."
—Dr. Alfred Velpeau, 1839, seven years before anesthesia was introduced

~~~~~

"The ordinary 'horseless carriage' is at present a luxury for the wealthy; and although its price will probably fall in the future, it will never, of course, come into as common use as the bicycle."
—*The Literary Digest*, 1889

~~~~~

"It looks, indeed, as if the next century, whatever it may have in the way of aerial flight in store for us, will have no difficulty, if it desires the honor, of being christened 'The Trolley Age'."
—*The Popular Science Monthly*, 1895

~~~~~

"Heavier than air flying machines are impossible."
> —Lord Kelvin, Royal Society, 1895

∿∿∿∿

"Everything that can be invented has been invented."
> —Charles H. Duell, director of the
> U.S. Patent Office, 1899

∿∿∿∿

"I must confess that my imagination, in spite even of spurring, refuses to see any sort of submarine doing anything but suffocating its crew and floundering at sea."
> —H.G. Wells, 1901

∿∿∿∿

"Is there to be an end of discovery and invention? . . . The Earth is nearly conquered now. We have reached the North Pole . . . and it has been proved that no one need go there again. . . . There are not likely to be any other great chemical or physical discoveries which will much affect the conditions of humanity."
> —"The Coming Era of Dullness,"
> *The Independent*, 1912

∿∿∿∿

"There is no likelihood man can ever tap the power of the atom."
> —Robert Millikan, Nobel prize
> winner in physics, 1923

∿∿∿∿

"While theoretically and technically television may be feasible, commercially and financially I consider it an impossibility, a development of which we need waste little time dreaming."

—Lee DeForest, American inventor and pioneer in radio and television, 1926

~~~~~

"Who the hell wants to hear actors talk?"

—Harry M. Warner, Warner Brothers, 1927

~~~~~

"There is not the slightest indication that [nuclear] energy will ever be obtainable. It would mean that the atom would have to be shattered at will."

—Albert Einstein, 1932

~~~~~

Expert Predictions About
People and Events

"Sensible and responsible women do not want to vote"

—President Grover Cleveland, 1905

~~~~~

"He Kept Us Out of War."

—President Woodrow Wilson's re-election campaign slogan, 1916, only months before Wilson and the United States declared war on Germany

~~~~~

"[Babe] Ruth made a big mistake when he gave up pitching."

>   —Tris Speaker, Hall of Fame outfielder, 1921

∿∿∿∿

"*Gone With the Wind* is going to be the biggest flop in Hollywood history. I'm just glad it'll be Clark Gable who's falling on his face and not Gary Cooper."

>   —Gary Cooper, 1938

∿∿∿∿

"I have no political ambitions for myself or my children."

>   —Joseph P. Kennedy, 1936

∿∿∿∿

"You'd better learn secretarial work or else get married."

>   —Emmeline Snively, director of the Blue
>   Book Modeling Agency, advising
>   would-be model Norma Jean Baker
>   (Marilyn Monroe), 1944

∿∿∿∿

"You ain't going nowhere . . . son. You ought to go back to drivin' a truck."

>   —Jim Denny, manager of the Grand Ole
>   Opry, firing Elvis Presley after one
>   performance, September 25, 1954

∿∿∿∿

"The thought of being president frightens me. I do not think I want the job."
—Ronald Reagan, governor of California, 1973

∼∼∼∼∼

Visions of the Future

Being employed as a prognosticator of long-term trends and events is an enviable situation. By the time it is possible to evaluate your degree of accuracy, you will be retired or a departee from this world. If your efforts are remembered at all, it might be with bemusement in a place like the Henry Ford Museum.

People are fascinated by experts' conceptions of the future, even though there is a high probability that the ideas will prove to be wrong. Walt Disney's Epcot Center in Florida attracts millions of people from all over the world who want to experience a simulated future now. Think tanks—organizations employing experts in various fields to construct future scenarios—find ready and willing clients in corporations and governments.

The World Future Society bills itself as "an association for the study of alternative futures." Through its publications, it forecasts and discusses the trends and technologies of tomorrow. *Omni* magazine was created in 1978 as "the magazine of the future." In the years since then, *Omni* has been true to its word by focusing its articles on the future and issuing forecasts of its own.

Consider a few more forecasts that I have selected from a number of sources, including the World Future Society and *Omni*. If you were an entrepreneur or corporate manager, how much would you stake on the strength of the forecasts? What commercial opportunities do the predictions imply?

A Sampling of Omni Forecasts

1997: A private school in California sets up the first classroom with coils to bathe students in a pulsed electromagnetic field while they work. Pulsed fields can aid or hinder memory, depending on the frequency and strength.

1999: After more than twenty years of work, scientists have almost finished mapping the sites of hereditary factors on the chromosomes within the cell nucleus. They predict that the effort will soon yield cures for such ills as cystic fibrosis, Huntington's chorea, and many forms of cancer.

2005: World water shortage grows.

2019: The consumer electronic rage this year is for new home robots. Budget models are little more than automated vacuum cleaners, but sophisticated units can set the dinner table, wash windows, make beds, and run security patrols at night.

2050: One million people now inhabit the solar system. Most live in space stations built of material mined on the moon.

A Sampling of World Future
Society Forecasts

The economy of Japan is in for a period of turmoil and decline during the 1990s. Japan will not regain its overpowering presence in world trade in the foreseeable future.

A worldwide economic collapse is extremely likely in the next few years.

In the next twenty years, microcomputing technology could reduce car accidents to 10 percent of current levels.

By the year 2000, the U.S. economy will generate $4 to $5 trillion of new capital assets, assets that will embody the next generation of applied technology.

A Potpourri of Forecasts

Robots will be so common in the workplace that there will be no jobs for humans in manufacturing, and human secretaries and receptionists will be considered a "perk" for executives.

When today's infants are adults, they will work twenty hours a week rather than forty hours; return to school at least once every six to seven years for occupation-related training; most likely live in Texas or California; purchase a first car that is ten years old with a lifespan of ten more years; face a 50 percent chance of divorce; and retire at age 75 or older.

A few of these forecasts will probably be close to accurate if for no other reason than chance alone, but many of them will be wrong. Lacking clairvoyance, humans cannot consistently determine which forecasts are close to being right and which are way off the mark. That is precisely why it is a blunder for entrepreneurs and marketers to put too much faith in forecasting. It is a gamble to count on a single forecast being right. Predictions are useful in stimulating one's imagination, but they are not something to stake the future on.

Stating Forecasting Assumptions

Any discussion of a hypothetical future that is to be useful for strategy purposes must include a clear articulation of its assumptions. A century ago, the famous retailer John Wanamaker made the often-repeated comment: "Half the money I spend on advertising is wasted, and the trouble is, I don't know which half." This candid admission of not knowing must have been more valuable for Wanamaker's advertising employees than if he had voiced no assumption at all. By stating the assumptions the forecaster allows others to see and know whether the predictions flow from reasonable assumptions. Weaknesses can be exposed, better assumptions substituted, and new and refined forecasts developed. This back-to-the-drawing-board approach takes more time than if forecasts are accepted without question. But the dialectical process can have two important results. First, it enables management to understand just how fragile a forecast may be. And second, it may change management's mind about preconceptions of its own and stimulate ideas for new and different business strategies.

Here is an example of what I mean. The financial vice-president of a major corporation had a bias against the use of advertising by his company: "We waste money on advertising. It has no effect on our sales."

Indeed, if you graphed the company's advertising expenditures and sales for past years, it did appear that there was no relationship between the two (see figure 5–1). But the company had not spent enough on advertising, so that its messages never reached most people or were lost in the noise and clutter in the mass media. In addition, its meager advertising dollars were scattered all over the United States and internationally, which meant that the advertising impact was further weakened.

The company then implemented a strategy of concentrating its advertising in major market areas where there were bright prospects for picking up share. It also significantly increased spending. Sales then began to respond (see figure 5–2).

The company's financial vice-president was partially right. The original advertising strategy was ineffective. The money spent on advertising had little or no effect on sales because the firm had not reached the spending threshold necessary to inform and persuade potential customers about the company's products. By testing alternative spending levels in several geographical markets, the company was able to approximate the amount it needed to commit to advertising in order to gain or hold market share.

Most predictions in business are based on straight-line extrapolations of past performance. But this assumption far too often goes unchallenged. Consider some of the paths that a trend can follow.

Premise: *"We waste money on advertising.*
It has no effect on our sales."

Figure 5–1. *Low Expenditure on Advertising*

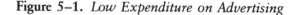

Alternative Assumption: *"We need to spend more on advertising and concentrate it in our major markets for impact. Once we pass a spending threshold, people will know more about our products and sales will respond."*

Figure 5–2. *Increased Expenditure on Advertising*

- *Grow like the universe.* This premise underlies the majority of the predictions made about trends. One theory of the universe holds that it is ever-expanding. Similarly, many companies assume that their growth line is linear and always rising. This manifest-destiny view of an ever-expanding industry makes companies vulnerable to displacement by new technologies and innovations.
- *Grow like a fish.* Like a fish, which continues to grow until it dies, a trend sometimes begins small and proceeds to inch along until it terminates. There is no leveling off and slow decline—just a prompt end. Slide rules achieved steady growth for years, and then they suddenly had none as hand-held calculators came on the market.
- *Grow like a teenager.* Instead of the smooth linear growth of a fish, a teenager often grows in spurts—and then abruptly stops. There is a ratchet effect for a while, and then no growth at all. Successive generations of in-home personal computers are likely to follow this pattern as aficionados buy them, a hiatus in sales occurs, college-educated households purchase them, another hiatus takes place, and so on until society reaches the saturation point.
- *Proceed like a falling object.* Some trends begin with suddenness, maintain high velocity, and end with the same kind of abruptness with which they began. Sales patterns for a hit movie, book, or song are examples.

It is a formidable and often impossible task to predict correctly what path a trend will take. The job is normally done with more confidence in mature industries, which have a long history of products and services to learn from. But even there, if a new technology comes along unexpectedly, an entire industry can be put out of business pronto. In the late 1960s, desktop calculating was done with typewriter-sized electromechanical machines that noisily and ponderously ground out the answers. These were relics a few short years later, along with many of the companies that made them. A person can now get almost instantaneous and noiseless answers from a calculator built into a digital watch.

In emerging high-technology industries with no past history, it is often anybody's guess whether a trend will emerge at all, much less what kind of growth path it will take. In these cases, venture capitalists and lenders want to see an explication of the assumptions and rationale on which the forecasts are based. Many times, however, both the investors and the entrepreneurs miss badly in their estimates of potential for an industry or market.

Gallium Gulch, California, is the source of a compound known as gallium arsenide, a material that can be used to make integrated circuit chips. In 1983, experts predicted that chips made of gallium arsenide would be a $2 billion industry, virtually supplanting silicon as the preferred material for high-performance semiconductor circuits. In 1986 and 1987, on the basis of this bullish outlook, venture capitalists invested over $300 million in gallium arsenide startup companies. By early 1988, for several reasons having to do with technical performance, the experts drastically altered their predictions. The revised outlook conjectured that gallium arsenide might eventually achieve a 10 percent share of the semiconductor market. The local gallows humor in Gallium Gulch is that the compound will forever be the technology of the future.

A company or individual's assumptions about the future need to be committed to writing and kept. An executive development exercise shows why. The instructor in a major company's executive training program asks the managers participating to write down their predictions and assumptions about what the next year will bring in economic activity, profits, politics, and other areas impacting business. These predictions are signed, discussed briefly, and then turned in to the instructor, who later seals them in individual envelopes. The instructor does not tell the managers that they will see their predictions again. One year later, the managers are reconvened and, without opening the envelopes, are asked to write down the predictions they made. Afterward, the envelopes are opened and comparisons made between what the managers actually said and what they think they said. Until the envelopes are unsealed and the comparisons made, the managers generally think that they were a lot more accurate in forecasting the one-year future than they were.

This training exercise demonstrates that unless there is a written record of both forecasts and the underlying rationale for them, memory bias can lead people to become dangerously comfortable with their ability to predict. Thus, they are unable to evaluate realistically where they went right and where they went wrong in planning or to learn from the experience.

All Customers Are Not Equal

The head of an engineering firm told me a story that illustrates what I mean when I say that all customers are not equal. This engineer had inherited the company from his father, who for decades had been a well known and highly respected civil engineer in the area of the state where he lived. The father's work had gained him the reputation of being a progressive and innovative builder.

Even so, late in life, in some respects he had difficulty coping with the electronic and software revolution that so impacted civil engineering. When hand-held calculators became commonplace, the father could occasionally be seen working a problem out with pencil and paper just to make sure the calculator was right. Later, when the engineering firm installed personal computers to help with surveying calculations, computational procedures, and accounting, the old engineer watched with awe and probably some trepidation as this alien technology performed. He never really trusted it.

It is well documented that customers are not equal in terms of their receptivity to trying and buying new products and services. People have different tolerances for risk. The engineer and his son might each have made the decision to equip their office with personal computers, but the son would have acted much sooner.

Some people never buy, particularly when a high-technology product is involved. A Washington, D.C., psychologist and several professors from George Mason University surveyed 462 managers and professionals. Eleven percent of the 462 were classified as computer-anxious; they avoided using computers whenever they could, but their anxiety might be overcome if they were to take a computer-training course. Three percent of the managers were called "cyberphobic"; they suffered physical and psychological distress in the presence of computers.

So some people buy new products early, some later, and some never. Those who do buy are classified as innovators, early adopters, early majority, late majority, or laggards, depending on when they make the purchase. As the labels indicate, the innovators are quick to buy a new product or service, and the laggards are the last.

An associate, Susan Higgins, and I researched the lifestyle characteristics of aficionados of high-technology products and services—individuals who are among the first to purchase camcorders, electronic security systems, satellite dishes, and other such gadgetry for their homes. We found that the innovators fall into three lifestyle groups, which we describe as Yuppies, Creators, and Purists.

Two common areas of interest form a bond among the three innovator groups. The first is an interest in sports of all kinds, encompassing both participation in sports activities and watching sports on television. The second commonality is an interest in investments, including real estate and stocks and bonds—which indicates a tolerance or possibly a preference for risk. The Yuppies have an affinity for gourmet cooking, fine foods and wines, and cultural events. The Creators like home and electronic do-it-yourself projects; they do their own automotive work and enjoy photography and stereo equipment. Gardening and growing plants are popular with the Creators. The Purists enjoy science and new technology for its own sake. They like videocassette recording, home computing, and video games. Their leisure activities also include biking, running, boating, skiing, and fishing.

Any high-technology consumer-products marketer who did not account for the lifestyle differences among these innovator groups in conducting marketing research and designing advertising strategy would be flirting with failure. And if these lifestyle variations exist among the three innovator groups, imagine what differences there must be between these risk-accepting innovative customers and the risk-averse laggards, people who wait and see and wait and see some more before finally buying that microwave oven or video-cassette recorder.

A company looking to market a product or service, or an entrepreneur wanting to start a new company, needs to be very careful in feasibility testing with potential customers. Customers differ in their tastes, preferences, lifestyles, and psychological makeup. If one asked people whether and when they would buy a new product, the answers given by innovators are likely to be much different from answers given by risk-avoiders. Often inaccurate predictions or forecasts are made because the underlying market research is not based on a random sampling. Ask a hundred risk-tolerant people to evaluate a new product; if 90 percent of them are effusive about it, that does not necessarily warrant an optimistic forecast about the product's commercial feasibility. The sample is biased.

On the basis of its declining U.S. sales in the 1970s, the Singer Sewing Machine Company would have had to conclude that it was in a dying business. But the United States, with its high percentage of working women who have less time to sew than they used to, is not typical of developing countries, where sewing is popular. At the same time that U.S. sales were decreasing, Singer found a more receptive market in the Third World. Again, all customers are not equal, and making predictions about what one group will do based on what another group says and does is hazardous.

Wildly optimistic predictions often arise from shoddy feasibility research. With gallium arsenide, R&D underestimated the technical obstacles. With market research, problems frequently stem from conclusions inferred from nonrepresentative samplings of customer opinion. I have seen entrepreneurs willing to risk everything to start a business because some friends, relatives, and acquaintances thought the entrepreneur had a "great" concept.

Worse yet, sometimes the entrepreneur thinks he or she has a great idea, but there is no evidence at all that it can be turned into a commercial winner.

Be a Non-Prophet Organization

J. Scott Armstrong of the Wharton School of Business at the University of Pennsylvania has found that objective studies of the stock market and predictions in psychology, economics, medicine, sports, and sociology do not promote better forecasts. Indeed, expertise beyond a minimal level is of insignificant value in forecasting change. Because people tend to ignore this objective evidence, Armstrong has proposed the "Seer-Sucker Theory": No matter how strong the evidence that seers do not exist, suckers will pay for seers.

Forecasting faith has led many executives and their companies down the garden path to new products and services that should never have been introduced and to flawed marketing strategies. Forecasting simply cannot be substituted for "what if" contingency planning built not around a forecast, but rather around several plausible and even a few implausible futures or scenarios. The development of winning marketing plans is a dialectical, free-wheeling, and largely qualitative process, not a mechanistic, rote exercise in number-crunching or blind adherence to someone's conjecture about the future—no matter who that someone is.

Experts in such areas as demographics, sociology, technology, international relations, and economics can be of considerable value to a company in sketching what they feel will eventuate in the future. But as the study by Scott Armstrong revealed, a company does not need to hire the Henry Kissingers or Milton Friedmans of the world to discuss the future—less well-known but competent individuals will do just as well. A Nobel laureate economist is not needed to discuss next year's inflation and unemployment outlook. If aspiring entrepreneurs or small businesses cannot afford advice, they may draw upon the wealth of published information at little or no cost.

Once marketers have enough information to speculate about several future scenarios, it is a matter of their undertaking "what if" games. It is like watching and reacting to the weather report on the late-evening TV news. The report says that tomorrow will be sunny and warm with little chance of precipitation. The prudent person will put a raincoat or umbrella in the car just in case. Likewise, the prudent marketer may expect one scenario but has rehearsed and is prepared for other eventualities. A common misperception is that successful entrepreneurs and entrepreneurial managers are riverboat-gambler types. They are not. They are calculated risk-takers, who do not bet on the even-money favorite, but neither do they bet on the long shot. A wager at 3-1 odds would be much more to their liking because it gives them a realistic chance to leverage their investment.

Questions to Ask Yourself

1. Are you convinced that no one can predict with any degree of consistency what the future will bring? How susceptible are you to the Nostradamus effect? Are you easily persuaded by pronouncements about the future from renowned experts? Do forecasts backed up with computer print-outs impress you? Are you a non-prophet organization?

2. Do you readily accept expert predictions and use them to formulate your objectives and strategies for the future, or do you view forecasts with a healthy skepticism and develop contingency plans? Do you inquire about and test the assumptions behind predictions? Do you state your own assumptions, preferably in writing, about the future so that others can point out what may be specious reasoning? Do you expect your sales to grow like the universe forever, like a fish until it dies, like a teenager in spurts, or like an object thrown off a tall building to the street below? Are your advertising expenditures unrelated to sales, or are you not spending enough to make any difference?

3. When you plan, do you engage in "what if" rehearsals? Do you outline the strategies that you might use in several alternative futures? Certainly, the strategies would be different for an economic recession or boom. What will you do if you do not obtain that big order you have been pursuing? What if you cannot find an investor to fund your proposed new business? What if the bank will not lend you money?

6
Blunder #5:
Practicing Chinese
Marketing

China's millions have bought many different things, and they have always been steady customers, they could always be depended on to absorb a good proportion of the world's surplus products.
—Carl Crow, *Four Hundred Million Customers*, 1937

C arl Crow was an Englishman who lived in China for years. He referred to himself as an advertising or merchandising agent, and from his advertising agency in Shanghai, he helped his international clients to sell everything from perfume to textiles to the Chinese. In his book *Four Hundred Million Customers* he gave rise to the term *Chinese marketing*. This came to mean business strategies based on preposterous assumptions about a company's ability to sell its offerings to vast numbers of people—with little consideration for anything else, such as consumer purchasing power or need. Crow apparently felt that the immense Chinese population—400 million in the 1930s—might "absorb" the world's "surplus," which was considerable during the years of the Great Depression.

There were two major problems with Crow's way of thinking. First, unloading surplus products on people is not marketing—quite the opposite. Marketers provide people with what they need and prefer, not with what someone has a surplus of to sell. Second, the existence of enormous numbers of people cannot necessarily be equated with untapped market opportunity. Islamic countries are not prime candidates for subscriptions to *Ms.* magazine, *Wall Street Week* would not be a long-running television program in the

Soviet Union, and liquor and cigarette companies do not have much of a market in heavily Mormon Utah.

Consider Carl Crow's reasoning for his proposed Apple-a-Day Club in late 1930s China. This scheme captured the very essence of Chinese marketing—self-deception and illogic.

> When working out figures of prospective sales it is best to be conservative, even when all the factors are so favourable that failure seems impossible, so we will assume that the advertising and sales campaign will not be an entire success, and that only half the people will become apple consumers. This will leave out the old who have lost their teeth, and the young whose dentition is incomplete and for whom orange juice would be more appropriate. Then, since one cannot expect rigid consistency in any human undertaking, let us assume that one half of the charter members of Apple-a-Day Club will not stick to the diet but get tired and discontinue it after the first month or so. Finally, in order to be thoroughly cautious, and arouse no false hopes, let us cut this conservative estimate of Chinese apple consumption from the orthodox regularity one might wish for, and assume that the remaining consumers will eat an average of an apple every other day. This would give us a daily consumption of fifty million apples, not an unreasonable amount for such a tremendous population once our advertising campaign has convinced them of the benefits to be derived. . . . Gosh, when you get down to details, the scheme is not practical. If all the British ships which call at Shanghai did nothing but carry apples they could take care of only a fraction of the business. Besides, if there were enough ships to bring them here, the Chinese railways and river boats couldn't haul them away. And also, if we sold all these apples to the Chinese, there wouldn't be any apples left for the rest of the world.

After working his way through these magnificent calculations, Crow obviously became uncomfortable with his own torturous reasoning and condemned his so-called conservative estimates of market potential by raising another obstacle:

> But, while a few [Chinese] are wealthy, the average purchasing power has been low, and a very small proportion has ever

become more than theoretical customers who are interesting for statistical purposes, but valueless from the standpoint of actual sales. It is doubtful if more than ten million Chinese could afford to buy an apple a day without diminishing their bowls of rice or noodles.

Carl Crow's grandiose kind of thinking can still be found today. It plagues many proposals for commercializing products and services. Moreover, in this high-tech age, the fallacious thinking of Chinese marketing is often obscured by page after page of impressive-looking computer print-outs predicting enormous sales to mass markets of customers. High-sounding technical esoteria and fancy computer projections can give Chinese marketing an aura of sophistication and validity. So Chinese marketing is more dangerous now than ever.

Commercial history suggests than an entrepreneur or company can and perhaps should think big—of that, progress and fortunes are made. But grand designs become unrealistic unless they are grounded in fact and objectivity rather than feelings and hope.

Bewitched by Big Numbers

"What if I could appeal to just one million people to send me a dollar? I would be a millionaire," someone thinks. Or, "If I send out 50,000 resumes, maybe just one company would be interested in hiring me for a six-figure income." How about this line of thought: "Wouldn't we do better advertising our golf clubs during the Super Bowl telecast than in *Golf Digest* because of the relative size of the audiences?" This mentality is based on the majority fallacy: The bigger the target market, the better—there is safety in marketing to numbers.

The great middle class in the United States and in other nations has encouraged Chinese marketing thinking. Marketers are tempted to look at the massive middle class—with all its purchasing power and its desire for goods and services—and conclude that if they could "only sell one-half of 1 percent of these households . . ." Effective marketers, by contrast, look not only at the numbers involved but also at the underlying consumer need or want for the product or service to be offered.

Direct-to-consumer marketers have a rule of thumb that mail solicitations average a return rate of 1½–2 percent. If one mails out, say, 10,000 brochures, there will be 150 to 200 takers for whatever is being sold. But these averages are misleading. Some solicitations may get a 6 percent response rate, others near zero. One direct marketer sent out 23,000 mail pieces for a forty-dollar product and received twenty-three orders. As an April Fools' Day stunt, Ron Chapman, a Texas disc jockey at radio station KVIL in Fort Worth, asked listeners to send in twenty dollars in cash, without mentioning why. KVIL's plan was to return the few hundred checks it expected to receive with interest, a package of treats, and a "Ha, Ha" note. In just three days of over-the-air promotion, KVIL received 12,156 legitimate checks, worth a total of $243,120. Kay Fishburn, a nurse in New Berlin, Wisconsin, has been orchestrating a direct-mail campaign to reduce the U.S. federal deficit by means of citizen donations. Ms. Fishburn's mail solicitation of 10,000 people, in the most recent year, contributed over $1.3 million to the Treasury Department's Fund to Reduce the Public Debt. An industrialist from Ohio contributed $100,000 plus his Social Security checks, and high school students in South Carolina mailed in $276.50 that they had raised from a car wash and door-to-door canvassing.

As these examples illustrate, the magnitude of customer response to a company's offerings depends on far more than sheer numbers. Whether the customer really needs and wants the products or services also counts heavily. A Chinese marketer usually has a good idea of how many people, by some stretch of the imagination might buy the product, but he or she badly miscalculates their desire to buy. In some cases, even the marketer's numbers are illusory. An organization calling itself the Maharishi Ayur-Veda Association of America actually placed a one-quarter-page advertisement in *The Wall Street Journal*, with the headline: "100 Billionaires Invited to Create a Disease-free, Problem-free Peaceful World Family—Heaven on Earth." According to the advertisement, each of the hundred billionaires would take monetary responsibility for caring for a population of fifty million people. The hoped-for response rate for this solicitation would surely have set some sort of record for converting superwealthy potential donors into actual donors, had it happened. But the world of the late 1980s has fewer than two hundred billionaires. Chinese marketing lives on!

Volume, Volume, Volume

Businesses make profit improvements in one of three ways: by increasing their margins, by increasing the volume of goods and services they sell, or—ideally—by doing both. The volume/margin combination can feed on itself. As a company attains additional revenue and market share, it often improves its profit margins as well. The concepts of "economies of scale" and "the experience effect" explain why.

Consider two competing manufacturers, company A and company B. Company A makes and sells 70,000 units annually, as opposed to company B's 30,000. Because company A sells so much more than its competitor, it can buy raw materials and supplies in greater quantity, thereby gaining a cost advantage from quantity discounts from vendors. Company A can also spread its overhead—white-collar salaries, depreciation on buildings, and other fixed costs—over 70,000 units, as opposed to company B's 30,000 units, again lowering its unit costs of manufacturing and giving company A an exploitable advantage. And that is not all. Company A's employees will probably be more cost-efficient at the actual manufacturing task than company B's, since they have over twice as much *experience* ordering materials, operating the production equipment, and maintaining and shipping inventory. So if that were not enough, company A may be able to afford superior production equipment because it is more profitable. In the terminology of business, company A will be "farther down the experience curve" than company B—a curve that depicts the relationship between a company's costs of manufacturing, on the one hand, and its experience in manufacturing, as measured by cumulative volume of output, on the other.

Study after study exploring the relationship between market share and profitability has found a high positive correlation between the two. The larger a company's market share, the better are its chances of being a return-on-investment leader among its competitors. This market share–profitability association is largely the result of the cost savings—and therefore improved profit margins—that high-market-share companies get from their business experience and economies of scale in manufacturing and marketing. This is not to say that small- and medium-market-share companies cannot be highly profitable. Sometimes, as a result of their agility and maneuverability in adapting to change, these market-share followers are able to earn a much better return on their investments than the market-share leaders competing against them. However, if one looks at a broad sweep of industries and companies, the high-volume companies will generally outperform their smaller competitors on return on investment.

This synergy between market share and profitability invites a corporate or entrepreneurial "volume mentality" and makes management susceptible to the foggy thinking of Chinese marketing. If a company can achieve volume and share, by all means it should consider doing so because of the unarguable boost that economies of scale and experience can give to profitability. But even so, management needs to ask whether the anticipated volume is realistically achievable or merely a long-shot stab in the dark. As the saying goes, "If wishes were horses, beggars would ride." The errors of Chinese marketing stem from management's wildly optimistic forecasts about market potential for a product or service and/or their underestimation of how forcefully competition retaliates.

Over a twenty-five year period, Du Pont Corporation spent $700 million developing its Kevlar fiber, which is lightweight yet five times stronger than steel. On top of this, it incurred heavy operating losses, perhaps $200 million. It was the largest investment that Du Pont had ever committed to a single product. That magnitude of expenditure in time and money requires volume selling. Du Pont had visions of the fiber becoming the sole material in tires, for example.

Kevlar has been used in a variety of products, from army helmets to golf clubs, but its sales and growth rates are modest for such a large investment. One Du Pont marketing manager for Kevlar said that the fiber was the solution for a problem—but no one knew for *what* problem. A market development team had to be formed to find applications for Kevlar.

This was virtually the identical problem that Du Pont had encountered with its leather substitute Corfam in the 1960s. Then, too, the company had to search for a commercial application for its product that had the potential for the vast volume that would justify its mammoth R&D investment.

Both these Du Pont experiences—Kevlar and Corfam—illustrate why Chinese marketing is so tempting. A company develops a technology at mammoth cost and then must search for commercial applications to yield volume sales. The company's marketers are placed under tremendous pressure to provide the answer, and in their zeal or anxiety, they become unusually vulnerable to making errors of judgment about market potential. The same goes for entrepreneurs and smaller businesses. Someone has an idea—maybe even a lifelong dream—for a new product, service, or business. As a consequence, this someone's vision may become blurred when it comes to forecasting the number of people who will become customers, as well as how much each customer will buy. The best time to ascertain a product's market potential is before it is far along in development, before the new product or venture is launched. Even high-tech companies with a strong commitment to R&D, like Du Pont, must, at some point in time and in the stream of monetary expenditures, demand hard facts concerning the key questions: Are there customers out there for this technological marvel? How many? How much will they buy?

The "Everyone's Going to Buy One" Snare

Employees spend most of their workdays somehow concerned with their employers' products and services. Executives design and implement business strategies, and nonexecutive employees do the making, selling, financing and transporting and perform other necessary tasks. Entrepreneurs, as well as many corporate employees, do not leave their work at work; they think about it during most of their waking hours and sometimes dream about it.

Time spent on the job causes a certain insularity. To some extent, a person's world is circumscribed by the people he or she meets doing business. This heavy exposure to people in a specific industry can and often does lead to the projection that customers in the broader world know more about a product or service than they really do—how much it costs, how high its quality is, where to buy it, and even the minutiae of its technical engineering. Since potential customers know these details, the thinking goes, they will certainly buy. They would be silly not to.

I once attended a two-and-a-half-day retreat at a resort at which executives of one company talked strategy and began to write a five-year marketing plan. It quickly became clear to me that these managers were vastly overestimating the general public's knowledge of and concern with the company's product line. Most consumers would not recall but one or two of the brand names in the product line, let alone make the technical and quality distinctions that the executives seemed to think they could. Customers do not want to commit much time to educating themselves about this particular product's intricacies, so they buy from a conveniently located retailer whom they trust, or else they purchase a heavily advertised "known" brand.

In the late 1970s and early 1980s, the "experts" were bullish and bold in their predictions for the in-home personal computer industry. Companies in the personal computer business talked in the parlance of the trade about bytes, bits, RAMs, DOS, booting up, and BASIC. Industry sales for personal computers doubled for several years in a row. It was heady stuff, indeed. Growth projections were in the lofty neighborhood of 60 to 70 percent annually, because "every household naturally must have a computer."

But someone had forgotten to ask the consumer—or else they did not listen—whether he or she would make the expenditure necessary to invest in a technology that would play video games, balance checkbooks, process words, store recipes, count calories, keep an appointment calendar, and help to make out a grocery list. How many people process words at home—what percentage of all households? Would the average American learn the software, with all its intimidating jargon? Selling high-technology products to the masses requires that a manufacturer disguise or mask the technology so that it is not intimidating, so that all the customer need do is push buttons or follow simple directions. Would the typical person take the time and make the effort to turn on a computer every time he or she needed to write a check? How long does it take to record and deduct a check by hand—with or without a seven-dollar calculator—in comparison with the time it takes to start up a computer and insert or call up the proper software?

Eventually, a large percentage of households in developed countries will have a personal computer—it will be like any other appliance. But this will not happen until the vast majority of consumers see a pressing need for a personal computer at home—probably as an accepted part of their telephone systems—and until the technology is truly "user friendly." Until then, most people will think like Rhett Butler at the close of *Gone With the Wind*—they will not give a damn about owning or leasing a personal computer to process words, keep recipes, or anything else along these lines.

Contrast in-home personal computers with videocassette recorders. The optimistic forecasts for sales and profits for VCRs came true because VCRs are technologically understandable by most people, are affordable to a majority of households, and offer obvious consumer advantages. Do most individuals and families devote more time to watching TV movies and other shows or to word processing? Moreover, camcorders, which enable a family to tape important events for posterity and to show them on VCRs, are considerably cheaper to own or rent than personal computers plus software. Comparing the perceived value of such high-tech appliances as VCRs, camcorders, and microwave ovens with that of personal computers, most households would and have opted for the former—hands down.

Management of one now-defunct small high-tech company was once certain they had a product that would be their ticket to success. It was a voice-stress detector, about the size of a hand-held calculator. Its red indicator supposedly lit up when it detected a stressed voice, and its green indicator came on for a relaxed voice. I asked one of the executives for a demonstration. She spoke, and the red light registered. She said that that was correct because she was in fact upset over her daughter's recent divorce. But several more of these demonstrations were unconvincing, to say the least. Management thought the market potential for this product would be enormous; they viewed the stress detector as a quasi–lie detector that one person, such as a purchasing agent, could use to see if another person, a sales rep, was comfortable with his sales presentation. Or a father might use it while quizzing an errant teenage son about his whereabouts the night before. As farfetched as this all seems, the founder of this company had made a small fortune from inventing another high-tech product, and when he talked, many people invested. His company ultimately went bankrupt after poor sales and trouble with the U.S. Postal Service for making medical claims (voice-stress analysis) while trying to sell the product by direct mail. Disgruntled investors sued the founder for misrepresentation, and the founder died during the controversy.

Some of the experts in the pay-per-view television industry based their initially rosy outlook for demand on the assumption that American television households—which are 98 percent of all U.S. households—would spend an average of ten dollars per month to view first-run movies and sporting events. They may be right—twenty years in the future. Less than half of all U.S. homes are cable subscribers. Of the forty million that do subscribe to cable, only five million have the equipment—the addressable decoder and sidecar—required to receive pay-per-view. And it costs $100-plus to install the equipment in each home. Already, pay-per-view has produced enormous one-night revenues, such as from the Hagler-Leonard and Spinks-Tyson boxing extravaganzas, but the industry is a long way from averaging ten dollars per month from all U.S. households.

The main cause of Chinese marketing is management's exaggeration of a product's value to the intended customers. When executives and entrepreneurs recognize that the products and services that seem so important to them are of but passing concern to many customers and of absolutely no concern to most other people, they have a start on improving their demand forecasting.

Several years ago, an ardent follower of a university basketball team was vacationing in Florida—over eight hundred miles from where the university is located. The team happened to be playing in the NCAA tournament, where it won an extremely close game in the final seconds. The fan had watched it on television in his motel room. Right after the game, he ran out into the lobby, excitedly shouting at the first people he encountered, "Did you see that?" "Did we see what?" they replied quizzically. Like this fan, enamored of his team and its performance, it's easy for management to project its own enthusiasm for its products and services onto prospective customers, who in reality may not care. That lays the foundation for Chinese marketing.

Pleasing a Majority of Customers
—But Which Ones?

Early in the industrial development of the United States and other advanced economies, there was little product differentiation. Coca-Cola, for example, was typical of how goods and services were supplied, not marketed, to the public in those days. Coca-Cola offered a certain size bottle of a cola-based, sugared product. Diet drinks, varied bottle and can sizes, and already-prepared cherry cokes were unheard of. Another example is Henry Ford's basic black Model T, the one that provided customers with two choices— to buy it or not to buy it. Later, as production capabilities improved, companies were able to supply customers and then some, which created plenty of competition. The one-product "supply" routines of companies like Coca-Cola and Ford were no longer possible. People wanted more, and if one company was not willing to give it to them, another would.

But it took a long time to reach that point. The world economy and wars kept interfering. In the Great Depression of the 1930s, many people could not afford to be consumers, let alone choosy consumers. During World War II, when the factors of production were devoted to making guns rather than butter, people were not much concerned with the quality of goods and services—not when compared to today. When gasoline is being rationed, one is thankful to receive an allocation and is not want to complain that it causes the car to make a pinging sound or to run sluggishly. Much of the world, especially Europe and Japan, was in shambles after the war, and it took time to rebuild, even with help from the Marshall Plan. Then the Korean War ensued, which diverted some production resources back to making war matériel. The era of modern marketing really began only after the Korean War, in the early 1950s.

The stage was set, for several reasons. For the first time in history, companies had the know-how, technology, and distribution capability to supply the goods and services customers needed and wanted. Just one occurrence—the building of the interstate highway system in the 1950s and 1960s—greatly improved companies' ability to deliver goods in a timely manner as never before. The war-ravaged countries rebuilt and became reindustrialized, and citizens gained unprecedented purchasing power.

Perhaps the most potent force was television. Television served to inform and educate so that the public became better consumers. People grew to be more demanding and less tolerant of high prices and inferior products, which is why Japan later became so successful in selling a host of products in the United States. Americans came to perceive that Japanese-made cars, electronic equipment, and other goods were better than the ones made domestically. Television began to have a homogenizing effect on the free world, which facilitated and led to the global business strategies we see today.

As a consequence of this affluence and of the fact that consumers could demand and generally get what they wanted in the way of products and services, companies were forced into a competitive strategy of market segmentation and targeting. The consumer became king. The adage "different strokes for different folks" became the prevailing theme for marketing strategy—at least for consumer-goods firms. Industrial or business-to-business marketers took a while longer to come around to this philosophy. Some companies never made the transition to the consumer-is-king philosophy and folded.

It is no coincidence that Ford Motor Company's classic failure with its Edsel came in the late 1950s, a watershed time in the transition of the U.S. economy from a production-orientation to a consumer-orientation. Ford had essentially tried to design a car that would please most people and ended up with one that pleased few people. After this expensive and embarrassing lesson, market segmentation of customers and careful tailoring of automobile versions to targeted segments became the norm in the industry. The pendulum swung from little customer choice in autos to too much choice—consumers became confused by all the models as the auto companies erred by oversegmentation.

Market segmentation and product positioning are strategic approaches to mitigate the risks of Chinese marketing. The marketer seeks to establish which customers and how many of them will buy what the company has to offer. What would be their motivations for doing so? This is a more customer-oriented approach than Chinese marketing, which simply says, "Look at all those people who are available to buy our product," without first exploring why they might want to buy.

In market segmentation, the marketer attempts to identify groups of people or businesses who have similar needs and preferences for a product or service. It subsequently tailors its products, services, and marketing programs specifically to these needs and wants. Concurrently, the marketer tries to position the company's offerings, via product/service differentiation, to appeal to customers more than those available from competitors. In dramatic contrast to the Edsel, the original Ford Mustang of the 1960s—which propelled Lee A. Iacocca to fame and fortune—was an enormous hit because it was unequaled in its close appeal to the transportation, style, and price needs of a huge segment of Americans.

Suppose a relatively new and unknown personal computer manufacturer is interested in selling its PC to people for use in their homes. The company, which I will call ONLINE, has a market research study that identifies five customer segments. The segments are based on two main dimensions—brand-name recognition and price (see figure 6–1). Segment 1 is the largest segment of customers. They prefer a moderately well-known brand at a moderate price, and they buy the IBM clones, such as the Leading Edge and Zenith brands. The next-largest segment is segment 2, customers who desire premium-price computers with high brand-name recognition, mainly IBM and Apple.

In this instance, a Chinese marketer would do one of two things. He or she would decide either to market the computer with one product and with one marketing program to appeal simultaneously to all the segments, or at the very least, to target the largest two segments. By contrast, a savvy marketer might conclude that all the segments are too hotly contested and there is little opportunity in any of them. Or that if ONLINE has any

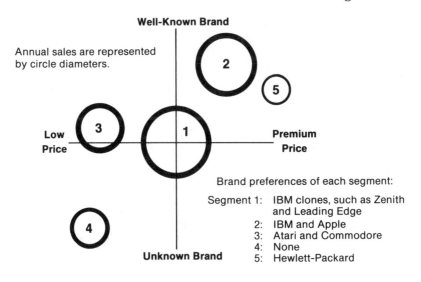

Figure 6-1. *Five Hypothetical Market Segments for In-Home Personal Computers Based on Price/Brand Preferences*

chance at all, it is perhaps in segment 3 or segment 4, two of the smaller segments but ones uncontested by IBM, Apple, and Hewlett-Packard.

Every marketer is confronted with trade-offs. In pursuing a mass-market strategy, based on selling to large numbers of potential customers, the marketer gives up some of the company's ability to cater to customer needs and wants. Yet, if the marketer caters precisely to individual customer needs, the company ends up selling to a segment comprised of one customer.

Which Strategy— McDonald's or Rodeo Drive?

What I call "the McDonald's marketing strategy" is founded squarely on a mass-market philosophy rooted in cost-saving standardization. Go to a McDonald's restaurant, and you will find customers ranging from unskilled laborers to professionals, all eating the same kind of food. And a McDonald's in California is basically the same as a McDonald's in Maine. Some of the great corporate success stories have followed this mass-market approach. Sears,

Roebuck expanded aggressively to the explosively growing American suburbs after World War II and was eminently successful. General Motors made its Chevrolet the car of choice for middle America. Major-league baseball and then later professional football achieved mass appeal across diverse income and social classes in the United States, as soccer did in Europe and elsewhere. Holiday Inn became a household name and a remarkable success by delivering on its promise to customers of no surprises—the rooms and services were similar regardless of location.

As consumers become more sophisticated, most companies find it harder to use the McDonald's marketing strategy. Even Sears began to lose some of its formerly loyal patrons as retailing became more fragmented. Sears was buffeted on one flank by discounters like K-Mart and more recently Wal-Mart, and on a second flank by boutiques and other specialty retailers, and on a third flank by upscale department stores. All these eroded Sears's customer following by catering more exactly to people's needs and desires. When Sears acquired the Dean Witter Reynolds stock brokerage firm, a question was asked that has a great deal of strategic significance: "Will people buy their stocks where they buy their socks?" Some do, but many more prefer to invest in securities through other brokers. A Dean Witter Reynolds office in a Sears store may be able to provide services equal to or better than, say, a Merrill Lynch stock brokerage office in a more fashionable location. But to many investors, the Dean Witter Reynolds office, positioned perhaps next to lawn mowers or major appliances, does not give off the same aura of professionalism and quiet competence.

The opposite of the McDonald's marketing strategy is what I call "the Rodeo Drive marketing strategy," named after the renowned street of ultra-exclusive and pricey shops in the Hollywood area of Los Angeles. In the Rodeo Drive approach to marketing, affluent customers are targeted with the best in products and services, and the object is premium profit margins. Groucho Marx is supposed to have commented that he would not want to be a member of any club that would let him join. That is the appeal of Rodeo Drive—exclusivity, association, and "the finer things of life." That is why gourmets and aspiring gourmets pay dearly for Wolferman's English Muffins, Silver Palate Sweet and Rough

Mustard, and Jamaica Blue Mountain Coffee. And in spite of what you hear, industrial purchasing is not immune to this kind of appeal. Corporations have been known to locate their headquarters in trendy parts of town that are not necessarily the best places for them to be from a purely cost-versus-benefit business standpoint.

Appearances do matter. If you ask a purchasing agent why he or she bought IBM personal computers for a company, you might get several utilitarian reasons in reply, when in fact the company simply may not want its visitors to see its employees using IBM clones, even if they are less expensive. In addition, a purchasing agent will sometimes tell you, in a moment of weakness, that "no one ever got fired for buying IBM." Buy IBM clones, have plenty of trouble with them—and see who gets the blame for being a penny-pincher.

These two strategies—McDonald's and Rodeo Drive—represent extremes and can be used by marketers as guides or frames of references for their own strategy formulation. Which way should a marketer's strategy tilt—toward middle America or toward Hollywood? Except for sellers of pure commodities, who have little opportunity for product or service differentiation, companies today are being forced by more sophisticated and demanding consumers to slant toward the Rodeo Drive tack. Even the big department store chains, which depend on mass marketing, are doing so. Federated Department Stores caters to divergent customer needs and wants not through one store but through a portfolio of stores—Abraham & Strauss, Bloomingdale's, Burdine's, Children's Place, and the like. General Electric sells the RCA and Hotpoint brands in appliances, as well as its own GE label. General Motors has a car for some nineteen major market segments.

Whether it is a large business or a small firm, the name of the game is usually market segmentation. Giant corporations seek volume by using several marketing strategies and programs to cater to the needs of multiple market segments. The medium-size-to-smaller companies dwell on fewer segments or even on only one. Marketing effectively to the generally knowledgeable, demanding, and increasingly affluent consumer of the modern-day industrialized societies necessitates this kind of precision in identifying and serving customer needs and wants.

A marketer begins to flirt with danger when it contemplates commercializing a product primarily because there happen to be a lot of people or firms who might buy. In considering market feasibility, the first question should be, Does this product or service meet a need or want? The second question should be, Does it fulfill this need or want better than our competitors' products and services? Then and only then ask, How many potential customers are there with the need or want? These inquiries can steer marketers away from pie-in-the-sky schemes like the classic Chinese apple-a-day strategy.

Questions to Ask Yourself

Is a mysterious spell known as Chinese marketing hexing the thinking of management or the entrepreneur? Here are some of the symptoms:

1. Is management so intent on recovering its investment in R&D, plant and equipment, and human resources for a project that marketers are almost frantically pressured to find a mass-market application? Put differently, does management have such an enormous investment in a technology or solution that it needs a ton of customers to recoup? If so, beware.

2. Is management so focused on driving down costs through economies of scale and the experience effect that marketers are forced to seek price-driven volume markets for largely standardized products? This strategy is appropriate for a commodity, but it is not likely to work for products and services in which consumers seek quality distinctions.

3. Does management or the entrepreneur think that the product or service is so outstanding that a certain percentage of the market is sure to buy? What evidence is there that this belief is warranted?

4. Is management planning to use a McDonald's standardized mass-market strategy for a product or service that actually requires narrow market segmentation and precise consumer targeting?

7
Blunder #6:
Confusing Financial/Marketing
Cause and Effect

Set short-term goals and you'll win games. Set long-term goals and
you'll win championships.
—Joe Paterno, head football coach, Pennsylvania State University

John Wooden, a sports legend, coached the men's basketball team
at UCLA for twenty-seven years. In his last twelve years there,
his teams won ten NCAA championships, seven of them in a row.
UCLA holds the record for the longest winning streak in any major sport—eighty-eight consecutive wins over four seasons. Coach
Wooden says, "Most people are surprised to learn that in twenty-seven years at UCLA, I never once talked about winning. . . . I
honestly deeply believe that in not stressing winning as such, we
won more than we would have if I'd stressed outscoring opponents."
If he did not stress winning, what did he emphasize to his players?
He emphasized preparation, teamwork, avoiding emotional peaks
and valleys, performing to one's level of competence, constant focus
on the future, and willingness to change.

Joe Paterno and John Wooden's insights are just as appropriate
for business competition as they are for athletics. In my view, a
championship performance in business is the achievement of getting and keeping a company highly profitable over a long period
of time. A championship performance is not taking actions that
will weaken a company for the future; it is not making a fast buck;
and it is not leaving someone else to deal with the mess.

Paterno says that to be a big winner, to become a champion, one
needs to eschew expedient short-term actions in favor of long-term

goals. Wooden would rather not talk about winning at all; he advises focusing on the fundamentals that lead to winning. This is sound advice, indeed, for entrepreneurs and for going concerns. Yet many entrepreneurs and even experienced executives confuse the cause-and-effect relationship between finance and marketing—between the score and how it is achieved. In winning companies, profitability is seen by top management as a *result* of market opportunity and marketing strategy, not as a *cause*. They know that financial rewards are by-products of long-term market strategies, not the other way around.

Fast Bucks

Every day, people and companies make large sums of money through savvy financial investing and finagling rather than by providing lasting value to the economy—funding new businesses and commercializing products and services. Unfortunately, at present federal tax laws favor short-term financial strategies over long-term investments. With no capital-gains incentives, the tax laws encourage such manuevers as the leveraged buyout—in which a firm is purchased with very little equity and a lot of borrowing—over the capital formation needed to fund technical and other entrepreneurial ventures. Why should venture capitalists invest in startup companies with possible long-term payoffs when they can make the more promising leveraged buyouts that have short-term payoffs? Either way, profits are taxed at the same rates. This is precisely why American entrepreneurs in high technology are seeking and getting funding from foreign interests. Foreign companies with money to invest are not as concerned with immediate return on their money as they are with having access to American technology.

In addition, the U.S. tax policy that did away with preferential treatment for capital gains has caused startup companies to have a harder time recruiting technical and managerial employees. Small companies used to be able to attract talent by offering stock as partial payment for services rendered. Then, when the stock was sold, any profits would be taxed at the more favorable capital-gains rate. No more. Now current income is taxed at the same rate as profit from stocks held over a period of time, which provides a compelling incentive to work for a large going concern and receive as much current income as possible.

In privately held companies, entrepreneurs and management have far more latitude to pursue long-term strategies that can build a company into a winner. Management in public companies is criticized for focusing on the short term, yet it is encouraged by tax policy to do just that. Companies like Kohlberg Kravis Roberts (KKR) can muster $40 billion to carry out a leveraged buyout or takeover. The companies they own most or part of—from Beatrice to W-I Forest Products—have annual revenues approaching those of General Electric. It is difficult for management to plan for the long term when a KKR may be in the hunt for the company.

Management by Watson or Icahn—
Take Your Choice

Winning businesses provide products or services that satisfy customer needs and wants better than the competition. These companies also do the right things now—such as search for better ways to build quality products—that will continue to keep them winning over the long haul. Winning companies know that competition is a marathon, not a sprint. Financial expediency for the purpose of short-term profit is not allowed to interfere with building a championship company.

Thomas J. Watson, Jr., built IBM into one of the greatest corporate success stories ever. Describing his strategy in the early boom years of the computer industry, Watson insisted that IBM's strategic goal was to gain and hold market position. IBM was to be a bold and broad-based competitor, thereby conceding no markets or niches to competitors. Watson said that any deviation from IBM's goal to gain and hold market position, such as in a misguided effort to optimize near-term profits, would have the effect of reducing the total amount of profit over the long term.

Contrast Watson's strategic vision with what occurred at TWA after it was taken over by Carl Icahn. Cash flow from operations improved under Icahn's management from $21 million to $306 million in only two years, as a result of lower costs, an aggressive push on Florida flights, and expansion of international routes. The per-share price of TWA stock doubled. So far, so good. But what about the long-term prospects for TWA? Its planes are noticeably the oldest of any U.S. carrier; and they are costly to maintain. TWA spent $76 million on capital expenditures in 1987, which was less than it spent in 1977. By comparison, in 1987, AMR Corporation and Delta Air Lines spent $1 billion each on capital expenditures, which was four times what they spent in 1977. TWA's long-term liabilities under Icahn grew to nine times greater than its equity, which does not augur well for replacing its fleet of planes. This precarious situation resulted from Icahn leveraging TWA assets—selling and leasing back planes and equipment—to gain cash needed to finance raids on USX and Texaco. In the two-year period in which TWA's cash flow mushroomed and its stock price doubled, its long-term debt and leases increased from $1.4 billion to $2.6 billion, while its cash and securities went from $169 million to $1.2 billion. When TWA purchased Ozark Airlines, it immediately mortgaged Ozark's fleet for $240 million.

There is a time for optimizing short-term return on investment—when an industry is declining, or when a company wants to phase out its participation in a line of business. However, if a company is to remain a strong competitor in an industry, management cannot make short-term decisions of expediency that mortgage the future. Would Watson or Icahn make the better chief executive officer for TWA if the choice were made on how well the company would be doing ten years hence?

Insufficient Capital

Inadequate capital is one of the major reasons why new business ventures fail. But more needs to be said. No amount of money can make a product or service successful if it does not fulfill customer needs and wants as well as or better than the competition. Capital does not by itself assure business success. Capital is important because it enables a new business to survive the high spending relative to sales that is necessary to develop the market and the company. A leading venture capitalist says that there are two reasons why new businesses fail—lack of sales, and lack of everything else.

This is not to say that financial considerations are unimportant or to suggest that a company should be spendthrift. New businesses in particular must have cash flow to survive. And financial controls are enormously important; companies fail when spending gets out of control. However, when management begins to talk and act as if the purpose of financial controls were to control the company, it has lost sight of what makes a winner—serving and satisfying customers better than the competition. Problems cannot be far away. It is customers and their needs that determine a company's fate.

Innovation and Risk-Taking

Rubbermaid's objective is for 30 percent of its annual sales to come from products that have been in its line for five years or less. In one five-year period, it introduced seven hundred new products. Similarly, more than 25 percent of 3M's worldwide revenues in 1987 came from products that were not in its line five years before. The same percentage of Johnson & Johnson's U.S. sales was from new products. More and more top managers have come to realize that innovation in the style of Rubbermaid, 3M, and Johnson & Johnson is what is required to compete in the rapidly changing world marketplace. But innovation cannot take place in a corporate culture where highly conservative attitudes toward risk-taking and by-the-numbers financial control stifle entrepreneurial *esprit de corps*. Rubbermaid's chairman, Stanley Gault, says that "in today's world, you just can't afford to be overly conservative." In his opinion, if a company has a 100 percent new-product success rate, it is too conservative. It should expect mistakes and learn from them.

James Burke is now chief executive at Johnson & Johnson. His first stay at Johnson & Johnson, early in his career, lasted only one year; he resigned, bored and frustrated by the centralized and stifling environment. On his departure, Burke suggested that Johnson & Johnson establish a new-products division, which it did three weeks later, and it brought Burke back to run it. One of Burke's first products, a chest rub for children, was a commercial dud. When Burke was summoned to the office of the big boss,

General Robert Wood Johnson, he thought his short tenure might be over. Johnson inquired of Burke if he was the one who had lost the company a great deal of money. Burke said yes. Johnson congratulated him and said, "If you are making mistakes, that means you are making decisions and taking risks." Johnson followed through on his belief that risk-taking is the way for a company to grow.

Innovative companies experience setbacks; that is an inevitable result of their aggressiveness. Even products that ultimately prove to be successful may look like failures at some point in their development-to-commercialization process. SmithKline Beckman, a pharmaceutical company with a deserved reputation for being highly creative in introducing new products, initially decided against marketing a vaccine that its scientists had developed for treating hepatitis. Nonetheless, the scientists persisted on their own, moving money from other projects to conduct clinical trials, and they finally convinced the company's international division that they should try the vaccine abroad. Annual sales quickly rose to $50 million, and the U.S. division promptly changed its mind.

Venture capitalists are accustomed to taking high financial risks. By providing capital for startup and growing businesses, they literally fund innovation. Venture capitalists expect to have about two significant successes out of every ten companies they invest in. But even with this high tolerance for risk-taking, they sometimes initially nix investing in what later turn out to be profitable ventures because they see them as being too risky. Investing in new business ventures is like trying to pick out which of the many ducklings on a lake will turn into a swan.

Take the company CPAid, a leader in providing a complete line of integrated software for federal and state tax preparation, tax planning, accounting, and record-keeping. The company's "electronic filing option" enables tax returns to be transmitted electronically from a user's personal computer to the IRS's computers via modem and telephone. CPAid was founded in 1978 in a small town in Ohio by Andrew and Helen Rosenberg. Their startup company became so successful that it was sought after by various companies as an acquisition target and was finally sold to Warren, Gorham & Lamont in 1987. This matter-of-fact progression from startup to success is a story of entrepreneurial risk-taking and perseverance.

Andrew Rosenberg has always been fascinated with technology. When he was in high school, he built an analog computer out of television test tubes. He later became an Air Force pilot and, after earning his CPA, began tinkering with software programming. In 1978, the Rosenbergs and CPAid introduced Master Tax, a software program for use in the preparation of federal tax returns. They set up a single tax preparation facility in a discount store in their hometown, where they began to use Master Tax, with a $9,000 investment in equipment. Revenues were so meager that the Rosenbergs' two partners left the business. But the Rosenbergs stayed with their fledgling venture until two occurrences put them on the road to success. First, personal computers became commonplace in the early 1980s, especially in numbers-oriented businesses like tax preparation. Second, when the Associated Press picked up on a story about Master Tax in the hometown newspaper, inquiries came in from all over the United States.

The Rosenbergs had been sure that their idea for computerized tax preparation would someday simplify and speed tax preparers' jobs. However, given their slim revenues in the discount store and the not-yet-widespread use of personal computers, confidence was not necessarily warranted. In 1978 or 1979, persuading investors of the market potential for Master Tax would have been a difficult achievement at best. It was not until personal computers became popular as a result of technological advances, price declines, and IBM's belated but powerful entry into the PC market, that suitors tried to invest in or buy outright the Rosenbergs' business. Considered from a strictly short-term, "bottom-line" orientation, in its early years CPAid was not a good financial investment.

In large companies, senior management cannot encourage risk-taking through psychology alone. The right attitudes and philosophies help to promote entrepreneurship, but they are not enough. The incentive compensation system must be aligned with a manager's mission. An executive given a new product line to bring to market should not be rewarded the same way as a colleague who is in charge of a declining line. The first manager's incentive compensation is tied to growth and future benefits, whereas the second manager's depends on short-term earnings. An incentive compensation system uniformly based on short-term return on investment discourages innovation and risk-taking. Even so, that is precisely how many companies reward their executives.

Investing in R&D, New Products, and Marketing

For a company that makes and sells tangible products, research and development and manufacturing are key ingredients in the recipe for a long-term winner. It is there that a company either does or does not develop and build the new and high-quality products that its marketers need to compete effectively. A company's marketers may be right on target in identifying commercial opportunities, but their alertness will be for naught if the products and services developed and manufactured are technologically behind the times or of poor quality.

The Strategic Planning Institute in Massachusetts has statistically analyzed operating and profitability information from three thousand lines of business contributed by 450 companies over a fifteen-year period. A truly significant contribution of its Profit Impact of Market Strategy (PIMS) program is that it has identified which strategic decisions lead to an increase in a business unit's short-term return on investment and which ones increase its value in the long-term. A "business unit," in PIMS terminology, is a division, product line, or profit center of a larger company. By "strategic factors," PIMS means such things as employee productivity, the extent to which fixed assets are used, market share, market growth rate, and plant capacity utilization. PIMS calculates a business unit's long-term value, or what it calls "value enhancement," using a formula based on the present value of cash flow from operations and appreciation or depreciation in the unit's market value over a five-year period. So in PIMS, "short-term" refers to less than five years and "long-term" to five years or more.

The PIMS program has found that nearly all the strategic factors that contribute to a company's short-term return on investment also contribute to its long-term value. However, the exceptions to this rule are important. Heavy spending on marketing and research and development and a high rate of new product introductions usually depress short-term return on investment. But in the longer term, this heavy spending and innovativeness enhance a firm's value. Likewise, although efforts to improve or maintain product quality detract from short-term return on investment, they are likely to elevate a firm's value in the longer term.

However, these findings do not mean that a strong monetary commitment by management to product innovation, R&D, and marketing will miraculously produce a rosy long-term future for the company—not by any means. Money can be spent wisely or unwisely.

The companies that spend heavily on research and have a high rate of successful new product introductions to show for it focus their R&D efforts carefully. The guiding philosophy behind this focus is market-driven. R&D projects are undertaken in response to a customer need or want. Successful innovation requires teams of individuals from R&D, marketing, manufacturing, finance, and legal who participate in research work from its outset. In market-driven R&D, the laboratory does not develop technology willy-nilly, and R&D is not allowed to proceed carte blanche. Marketers are not seen merely as people needed to find a use for laboratory discoveries in the form of a product or service.

Marketing expenditures should also be focused on the job at hand. A shotgun approach to spending for marketing says, in essence, that management has little idea about which media and creative appeals are most effective in selling its offerings. It is not unusual that a company is willing to spend big dollars to promote its product or service but is unwilling to fund the market research needed to indicate where and how the promotional dollars can be used most effectively. This false economy leads management to throw up its hands and say, "Look at all the money we spent on advertising and promotion, to no avail. Promotion doesn't work well for us."

If management wants to boost long-term profitability, it spends heavily on marketing, R&D, and product quality pursuits. It encourages entrepreneurship by sending the right psychological signals and by installing compensation systems that differentially compensate managers according to their missions. But this spending and quest for entrepreneurship are done in a highly focused way, with clear market and marketing objectives in mind. Executives seeking to perpetuate a company do not mortgage the future by emphasizing short-term financial considerations at the expense of market development.

All kinds of good things happen to innovative and market-driven new-product companies. The spin-offs from having a market focus and being aggressive in introducing new products are considerable. Rubbermaid, although it did not sell rubber gloves, read in a consumer survey that the respondents thought it was the number-two rubber-glove manufacturer and marketer. Seizing upon this opportunity, the company began selling rubber gloves in 1988. Consumers had also previously ranked Rubbermaid high in microwave cookware and food storage containers—before the company actually sold these products.

What About Service Businesses and Middlemen?

Nonmanufacturing businesses are generally not concerned about doing laboratory R&D. Retailers and distributors buy what they sell, and service businesses have no product as such. Nonetheless, companies like Lands' End and L.L. Bean in direct-to-consumer selling, Federal Express and UPS in overnight package delivery, and The Limited in retailing stay ahead of the competition through innovativeness in applying technology. Although these companies do not engage in R&D in the same way as, say, Eli Lilly, John Deere, and Digital Equipment, they do research customers and develop innovative marketing programs to meet their needs better than the competition. The Limited, for example, has one of the most responsive inventory-ordering systems anywhere, and Lands' End is recognized for its ability to use technology to process orders.

Smaller companies that are innovative usually work smarter than their larger competitors rather than trying to outspend them. The president of a profitable printing company proudly accepts the appellation "revolving junkyard" for his firm. Instead of tying up large sums of money in printing presses based on the latest in technology, his company buys used presses, "soups them up" so they will run at 110 percent capacity, and keeps them going with little downtime, over three shifts a day if necessary. By innovatively avoiding some of the high fixed costs and capital intensity of the printing industry, and substituting mechanical knowhow, the company produces a quality product at a competitive price in a highly price-sensitive industry.

Promotional Expenditures and Sales

Lee A. Iacocca, describing the attitude of Ford Motor Company financial executives during the troubled 1970s, when he was company president, commented, "While their company was dying in the marketplace, they didn't want to make a move until next year's budget meeting." Iacocca said that the financial managers felt it was their mandate and duty to save Ford from the radicals who wanted to spend the company into oblivion.

For the vast majority of companies like Ford, the two most important determinants of short-term sales levels are the state of the general economy (or the economy of a particular industry) and the amount of money spent on advertising and promotion. Executives have no control over the economy, but they surely do have control over promotional expenditures. Yet, illogically, the favorite target of budget makers and controllers is often advertising and promotion, especially in times of economic downturn, although in fact those are among the last areas that should receive the budget ax. Indeed, a strong case can be made that expenditures for advertising, sales promotion, and personal selling should be *increased* in bad times rather than cut—in absolute dollars as well as in percentage of sales.

This kind of circular reasoning creates conflicts, like the one described by Iacocca at Ford, between marketers and financial controllers. A popular computational technique for setting the advertising and promotion budget is the percentage-of-sales method. Say that for a certain company this year's revenues turn out to be $1 million, and the company spends its usual 2 percent of sales on promotion. Thus, its budget for promotional activities is $20,000. Management sees an economic downturn coming next year, with company sales sliding to $800,000. Using the percentage-of-sales method and applying the company's usual 2 percent, the promotion budget will be $16,000.

This example shows why a mechanical-formula approach to spending for marketing is inadvisable. Sales revenues depend in part on how much is spent for advertising and promotion; or put another way, sales is a function of promotion. The percentage-of-sales method has it backward—that promotion expenditures depend on sales levels. It is impossible to project that next year's sales will be $800,000 without first knowing how much the company intends to invest in advertising and promotion, unless the promotion is totally ineffective. If that is the case, why bother to advertise at all? Maybe the company in this example should spend $20,000 or more next year, thereby perhaps increasing the percentage of sales committed to promotion.

This kind of countercyclical advertising—in which a company increases the promotion budget as a percentage of sales in bad times—is now widely used by the automobile companies. The main promotional tactic they rely on when sales are slow is price rebates. However, the tendency in most organizations is to take the financial scalpel to advertising and promotion when tough times set in. But cutting the promotional budget only exacerbates the decline in sales, which is reason enough for management to avoid across-the-board budget cuts in troubled times.

When John Sculley arrived from Pepsi-Cola to turn around the declining Apple Computer Company, one of the first strategic moves he made was vastly to increase the company's advertising budget. Despite grumbling and objections from many employees, who thought technology alone was enough to sell computers, Sculley placed advertisements in such costly spots as the Super Bowl. It worked!

Managers of small companies and entrepreneurs are inclined to use what amounts to a "what-we-can-afford-to-spend" approach to budgeting for advertising and promotion. Like the percentage-of-sales method, this is no way to set the promotional budget. For the vast majority of companies, advertising and promotion are not discretionary items; they, more than any other area under management's control, can affect the immediate level of sales. As the venture capitalist said, lack of sales is the main reason companies fail, and lack of everything else is the next reason.

Lotus Fever

Walter R. Lovejoy was formerly a high-level planning strategist at Beatrice Companies; he later became the head of a company acquired from Beatrice in a leveraged buyout. At Beatrice, he found two distinct kinds of nonplanners: entrepreneurs who stored everything in their heads, and business-school-trained professionals who believed that planning was an exercise on their calculators. Lovejoy developed a planning process built around challenging, thought-provoking questions instead of around numbers. For example, marketing managers might be asked about the age of their products, their future product mix, their competitors' strengths and costs, and what they would do if they lost their biggest account.

I know what Lovejoy means. At a seminar on strategic market planning for the commercial banking industry, one of the bankers expressed disappointment that there was no planning software discussed—a sure sign that this individual was an operations type rather than a strategist.

One of the prevalent conceptual errors in business plans, whether they are written by people in going companies or by fledgling entrepreneurs, is that the strategies described do not have the remotest correspondence to the financial projections. Look initially at the strategies, and then examine the pro-forma cash-flow estimates, the income statements, and the balance sheets. Try to fathom how the glowing and Pollyanna-like future predicted by these financials will result from the strategies.

Robert J. Crowley, vice president of a state-owned venture-capital firm, the Massachusetts Technology Development Corporation, says that there is a disease that affects writers of business plans called spreadsheet-itis. For instance, Crowley received an afflicted ninety-eight-page business-plan funding proposal that contained forty-eight pages of spreadsheets. He and other venture capitalists blame word processors and spreadsheet software for such rambling, unfocused plans. Burgess Jamieson, of the California venture-capital firm Sigma Partners, says that the popular Lotus 1-2-3 spreadsheet is contributing to the poor quality of business plans. The business-plan writer can generate all kinds of fancy financial projections, yet have little grasp of their degree of realism.

Even Benjamin M. Rosen, who funded Lotus in its startup stage, believes that spreadsheet analysis has made it too easy to crank out financial forecasts.

One venture capitalist whose business it is to read and evaluate business plans says, "The standard business plan usually shows losses the first two years and then a doubling of profits every year after that. If hard thinking does not accompany the business plan, I tend to discount the financial section. The entrepreneur does not understand what the software has generated . . . because he or she has not worked through the numbers." Another investor remarks that he wants to see an entrepreneur's numbers worked out by hand rather than on a spreadsheet software program. Still another venture capitalist requires an entrepreneur to submit a floppy disk of spreadsheet-generated pro-forma financial statements for—and only for—the "most likely" projections. Then the venture capitalist is able to use the floppy disk to run his own sensitivity analyses using different assumptions about sales and expenses. As another venture capitalist remarks, "A financial strategy can be designed for any point in time. If a company does not have a product and market, nothing can help the financials because it is a derived function."

Spreadsheets tend to encourage the thinking that financial strategy is the cause and that market and marketing strategy are the effect. My own view is that spreadsheet software is useful in exploring the possible financial outcomes of various market strategies under one or more economic scenarios, as long as the person doing the simulation understands and states the assumptions behind the numbers. However, I am skeptical when I see page after page of output with no stated assumptions or explanation of how the financials derive from strategy.

One would-be entrepreneur was proud of the job he had done in putting together a proposed budget for a new business using one of the popular spreadsheets. His budget did look professional. But he could not explain it. Moreover, the budget apparently was not derived from the market strategy he had mapped out elsewhere in his business plan. This kind of situation is not confined to entrepreneurs; spreadsheet software users in large companies often do the same thing. It is the ease of use that makes spreadsheets dangerous, particularly in the hands of financial novices.

Allegis-ized in America

Plenty of money can be made through investing. So-called corporate raiders ply their trade by moving against what they believe are undervalued companies. But the raiders make profits by selling off assets, finagling, speculating, coercing, engaging in proxy fights, and other financial maneuvers. They do not create new products and services. Corporate raiding is not entrepreneurship, and it does not create new wealth.

Some of the companies that become the targets of takeover attempts richly deserve it. They have grown bureaucratic and inefficient, and generally their top executives are not good guardians of the stockholders' investment. In most of these cases, management is inept and more concerned with perpetuating itself than with doing the things that will make the company grow and prosper. For example, one of the better-known corporate raiders toppled a corporate chairman who was using the company's hunting lodge and jet as if they belonged to him and his family. The raider failed in his efforts to get control of the company. But by calling attention to this personal empire, the raider persuaded the board to force their CEO out, and the stockholders benefited. In other cases where a takeover is deserved, incumbent management has widely diversified into areas far beyond its strategic competence, thereby diverting resources from the company's core business and eventually weakening it.

Revlon is a good example. The cosmetics company that Charles Revson built had the leading market share in its industry when he died in 1975. Ten years later, Revlon had slipped to third or fourth in market share. Between 1981 and 1985, its profits declined by 60 percent. Revson's immediate successors had diverted resources from the cosmetic lines to fund investments in health care. Ronald Perelman won the company from them in a hostile takeover and took it private. He began to sell off the health care businesses and rejuvenate the cosmetic lines. Under Perelman, Revlon spent heavily for innovative and bold advertising around the theme "The world's most unforgettable women wear Revlon." Its Fire and Ice lipstick and nail polish campaign featured tigerish-looking models. Perelman introduced new products, reformulated old ones, undertook store promotions, repaired Revlon's relationships with retailers, and acquired the Max Factor and Yves Saint Laurent fragrance lines. Perelman turned out to be just the doctor that ailing Revlon needed.

But in other cases, corporate raiders go after companies that arguably may not deserve to be picked on—companies with reasonable plans for ensuring future prosperity. Take Allegis, formerly United Airlines. In a fly-drive-sleep strategy, Allegis had become a travel company, owning United Airlines, Westin Hotels, Hilton International Hotels, Hertz, and several other travel-related subsidiaries. But the costs of putting this strategy in place were a drag on Allegis's earnings. In turn, its stock price sank to below the breakup value of the company—and the raiders were quick to act. Consequently, the long-term effectiveness of the fly-drive-sleep travel strategy never had a fair chance to prove itself.

Three individuals calling themselves Coniston Partners accumulated 13 percent of Allegis common stock and, in effect, demanded that Allegis chairman Richard Ferris reverse his market strategy. Coniston threatened to sell its stock to the pilot union at United Airlines and to launch a proxy fight to replace Allegis's incumbent board of directors. Faced with this possibility, the board of directors relented, fired Ferris, ultimately dismembered the company, and changed the name from Allegis to UAL. About all that could be said positively for this raid is that "Allegis" was an awful name in need of change.

So a major reason that chief executive officers in publicly traded companies are inclined to emphasize short-term financial issues over long-term market development strategies is fear of being raided. For instance, *Business Week*, which tracks R&D spending by U.S. companies, has found that the wave of corporate restructurings in the late 1980s and the emphasis on short-term profits pushed "R&D spending back into the doldrums of the mid-1970s."

Even so, from a regulatory perspective, there is a dilemma. Many federal and state government provisions that would curtail corporate raiders from taking over a company like Allegis, a company planning for the long haul, would also entrench inefficient management in companies like Revlon before Ronald Perelman got control and rehabilitated it. The result would be that the economy would lose much of its ability to continually renew itself.

There would be less competition and far fewer opportunities for new industries and young companies to replace older, unresponsive ones. Antitakeover laws favor the status quo and stifle innovation.

However, if top managers of U.S. companies are to be encouraged to emphasize long-term market development strategies over short-term financial considerations—a must in global competition—some tinkering with federal fiscal policy incentives and security laws is needed. A study by the RAND Corporation makes it clear that the United States is not in decline, contrary to what some would have us believe. For instance, the U.S. economy's share of the global product is about the same now—22 to 24 percent—as it was in the mid-1960s. Still, this does not mean that no improvements are needed. A study by the nonprofit Council of Competitiveness developed a new four-item index to measure U.S. competitiveness in the global economy. The United States, although still strong, is losing ground to other industrial nations on all four items in the index—living standards, trade, worker productivity, and investment in education, R&D, and new plants and equipment.

Why not install a highly favorable tax rate for capital gains on stock held, say, for three years, a still lower rate for those on stock held for five years, and little or no tax rate at all for capital gains on stock held for at least ten years? This kind of sliding scale for taxing long-term capital gains would encourage stock ownership in the historic sense of investment and discourage trading. At the very least, capital gains profits should be indexed to inflation so that an investor pays taxes on real profits, not illusory ones. If Mr. or Ms. Citizen buys a stock today at $100 per share and sells it in three years at $120 per share, he or she should not be required to pay taxes on the portion of the $20 of profits that is nothing but the result of a rise in the overall price index.

How about a 50 to 60 percent tax rate on the dividends and short-term capital gains of stocks bought and sold within a year? Some traders, notably Japanese insurance firms, buy and sell American stocks within a two-hour period—just long enough to get the quarterly dividends.

Why permit greenmail, in which a company buys out a corporate raider at a premium over the going price of the company's stock and treats the rest of the stockholders as second-class investors? Why invite a raider in with this kind of incentive?

Compare the way small and growing companies in the United States and Japan issue initial public offerings of stock. In Japan, stockholders who agree to hold the stock of an issuing company for a long duration, usually ten years or more, receive a 30 percent discount from the public offering price that everyone else pays. This system ensures some stability in ownership for a young company. By contrast, in the United States, a trader who buys shares in an initial public offering can sell them immediately. The Japanese system gives young companies more freedom to build long-term strategies around heavy spending for R&D and marketing. Management has some breathing room. Investors are afforded the opportunity to buy-in—at a 30 percent discount—to a possible growth company whose management can pursue winning long-term expansion strategies without looking over its shoulder for corporate raiders.

Sales-CEOs Redivivus

In novelist John Updike's best-seller *Rabbit Redux*, the word *redux* is a shortened version of *redivivus*, which connotes that something has been brought back, as from poor health, or reborn. *Redux* is an appropriate way to describe what has happened to the esteem accorded to sales people in all kinds of business organizations. In the early days of American industrial development, heads of leading companies whose backgrounds were in sales were commonplace. In fact, some of the founders of today's premier companies started out as peddlers. Later on, as the art of running an organization took on a more scientific aura, sales employees in many corporations were considered as valuable infantry-type foot-soldiers carrying out orders on the front lines of commerce, but were not really the people with the vision and financial acumen to make generals.

In some organizations, selling was considered something of a necessary evil. Malcolm S. Forbes, editor-in-chief of his namesake magazine, recalled a conversation he once had with the then-chairman of one of the prestigious money-center banks. Forbes asked the chairman something about the bank's advertising. The chairman replied, "As chief executive here I don't involve myself in the bank's selling efforts." Forbes's reaction? "Incredible, eh?"

This thinking has changed. Selling is back as a promising career path to the top of a corporation. Many of the chief executive officers of the leading corporations around the world worked their way up the organizational ladder through sales.

Sales-CEOs are even more noticeable in smaller, high-growth companies. A survey by *Success* magazine of 150 of the United States' fastest-growing businesses found that 37 percent of them were headed by chief executive officers from sales backgrounds. In addition, the smaller the company's annual sales were, the greater the likelihood that the CEO had a sales background: sales and entrepreneurship go like hand and glove. Sixty-five percent of the companies whose primary business was wholesaling or distribution were run by a sales-CEO. In retailing, 45 percent of the CEOs came from sales. Fifty percent of the manufacturers had sales-CEOs, and 24 percent of the service firms. Of the high-technology manufacturers, 27 percent of the CEOs had sales experience. In computer companies, the figure was 35 percent, and for biotechnology firms it was 21 percent. *Success* also confirmed that many Japanese companies have people with sales backgrounds in top-level posts, some in the CEO position. The Japanese like the perspective on what makes a business go that a selling background instills in a person.

What do sales-CEOs offer? Empathy for customers, face-to-face experience in listening to and solving customer problems, interpersonal skills, drive, a competitive spirit, and an ability to take rejection are all characteristics of people who succeed at selling—traits that can serve a CEO well. Sales-CEOs are apt to put customers above short-term financial expediency. Of course, there are also potential liabilities. A sales-CEO may be so sales-oriented that he or she pays too little attention to profitability.

The main reasons why former sales employees are in renewed demand in the executive suites of corporate America are their experience with customers and their experience with solving customers' problems. People who have been effective sales representatives are entrepreneurial sorts. They know firsthand that the key to success in business is satisfying customer needs and wants better than the competition. They know that if a company can do this consistently, the financial rewards will follow.

Questions to Ask Yourself

1. In your company, are the financial controls too rigid? Are they stifling management's capability to adapt to marketplace changes and stay ahead of competition? Or are the financial controls so lax that the company is spending itself into problems?

2. Is making lots of money the be-all and end-all in your company, or is making money seen as a natural consequence of beating the competition in satisfying customers? People who start businesses primarily to "make money" usually fail because the focus is on the entrepreneur rather than on the customers and their needs.

3. Is Lotus 1-2-3 fever, the infectious spreadsheet-itis, rampant in your company? Have you and your managers carefully considered the financial statements and their assumptions? Do you know whether and how they accurately reflect your market strategy and position?

4. Does your company mortgage its future by emphasizing short-term profits at the expense of spending on the activities contributing to longer-term market development and financial worth—R&D, product/service innovation, and marketing?

5. Is your company's advertising and promotion budget one of the first areas to receive the budget knife in economic downturns? Lack of sales is the main reason businesses fail, and lack of everything else is the other reason.

6. Does your company encourage risk-taking and entrepreneurship by words and actions? Are product failures penalized? Do you tailor managers' financial incentives to the job at hand, or is everyone compensated on short-term return on investment?

7. Is the head of the company actively involved in sales strategy?

8
Reducing Risk

Chance favors the prepared mind.

—Louis Pasteur

I n tightly controlled laboratory experiments in chemistry and physics, certain inputs invariably produce known outputs. But in marketing strategy, causes and effects are problematic. In the marketplace are many economic, political, and social occurrences that are beyond management's ability to know and control. How buyers will react to a company's offerings cannot be predicted with certainty. And they might react one way today and another way tomorrow, depending on prevailing circumstances and their moods. People are not automatons and therefore only probabilistic statements can be made about how they will behave.

Marketing strategy formulation is more art than science. Two managers with exactly the same amount of money to spend on marketing may get very different outcomes because skill in making the allocations plays a vital role.

Mistakes in strategy are inevitable because of the inherent risks in the marketplace and in the art and science of formulating marketing strategy. Any company that does not make mistakes is too conservative. A strategist, however, should not beat himself, so to speak, by taking any more chances than are necessary. The risks associated with the six classic and timeless marketing blunders can be reduced.

Blunders: Building Better Mousetraps
and
Practicing Chinese Marketing

Symptoms: Optimism or even euphoria by the entrepreneur or management about the commercial future of a technology, product, service, or business venture, without the objective buyer research and analysis of competition to warrant it.

Appropriate Risk Reducer: An obsession with buyers, their needs, and competitors.

Listening to Customers

The only way for companies and individual entrepreneurs to mitigate the risks of building products or developing services that fail commercially is for them to be obsessed—yes, obsessed—with buyers and with competition. By knowing customer behavior and needs inside out, management will lessen its chances of making wildly optimistic estimates of market potential.

Defining who "the customers" are is the first step in learning about their needs, wants, and problems, in developing winning products and services, and in making more accurate estimates of the market potential for them. Most attempts to define "the customers" yield several possible groups. The whole idea behind market segmentation is to somehow classify buyers with similar needs so that they can be catered to with marketing programs tailored for them.

Ignoring Satchel Paige

Satchel Paige, the legendary baseball pitcher, is known for his advice, "Don't look over your shoulder, because someone might be gaining on you." This is bad counsel for companies. Better advice came from the original John D. Rockefeller, who said that next to knowing your own business, knowing about your competitors is most important. It is not enough to satisfy customer need; you have to do it better than the competition. To a certain healthy degree, successful companies that are able to sustain their prosperity run scared of competition. A little paranoia about what the competition is or might be up to avoids the complacency and smug satisfaction that invite trouble.

Keeping abreast of customer needs and competitors is a never-ending task. What customers want now can change in short order. What competitors are capable of delivering can change with the next technological breakthrough, innovative service concept, or strategic alliance via joint venture or merger.

The purpose of market research is to provide management with insights about customers and competitors. To be effective, it requires both quantitative and qualitative methods.

Statistical and Qualitative Analyses

The quantitative methods of statistical sampling and inferential statistics permit a company to make generalizations. A classic error in political polling occurred in the 1936 presidential election. *Literary Digest* had used the results of a telephone survey to project that Republican challenger Alf Landon would defeat Democratic incumbent Franklin Roosevelt by a landslide. But in 1936, telephone subscribers were disproportionately Republican. Twelve years later, the polls missed again by forecasting that Thomas Dewey would turn Harry Truman out of the White House. The pollsters quit surveying voters a week before the election, and many undecided voters made up their minds for Truman in the days immediately preceding the election. Today, pollsters have vastly improved their forecasts, with random sampling of voters right up through Election Day itself.

These examples of nonscientific surveys that produced inaccurate predictions have plenty of implications for companies. Survey a nonrepresentative sample of potential customers, and you run the risk of receiving the wrong signals. You may be told you have the greatest product since the wheel, only to find later in the marketplace that inadequate sampling led you to an Alf Landon–type error.

Advances in statistics—particularly what are known as multivariate statistics—and in computer power to run these programs can reveal insights about buyer behavior that are missed by the human eye. This capability has improved companies' ability to segment markets and to design products and services that meet customer needs more precisely.

One of the dangers of amateur market and customer research is that a nonrepresentative sample will be drawn, ultimately leading to the wrong conclusions. A second danger is that, even if a representative sample is used, the amateur market researcher will not be versed in the multivariate statistics needed to search for complexities.

Entrepreneurs and small business people who cannot afford the services of a professional marketing researcher have several alternatives. Secondary information sources published by government, trade associations, and syndicated market research services are available in many large public and university libraries. For instance, the Akron, Ohio, public library has an entire section devoted to small business that emphasizes information about bidding for government contracts. Appropriate college and university classes will sometimes work with an entrepreneur or small business if the project helps the students learn. However, this is like going to a dental school clinic to have the students work on your teeth. The cost is less than going to a licensed and experienced dentist, but the job they do may or may not be as good.

This is not to say that paying more for market research necessarily assures higher quality work. The thought to keep in mind about hiring market researchers is that the occupation does not require a license. Anyone—from a skilled professional to a charlatan—can use the title. Ask about the academic credentials and experience of the market researcher you might retain. Ask for some references of former clients—and call them.

For customer research, the quantitative approaches of random sampling, surveying by questionnaire, and analysis via inferential statistics rarely suffices. Buyer behavior is too complex. In-depth qualitative research usually adds valuable perspectives. The McCann-Erickson advertising agency once interviewed some low-income southern women about insecticide brands. These women were adamant that a roach killer that came in plastic trays was more effective and less messy than roach spray in a can. The women, however, would not buy the product in the plastic trays but were strongly loyal to sprays. McCann-Erickson, searching for an explanation for the obvious contradiction, had the women sketch pictures of roaches and compose short stories about them. Paula Drillman, the director of strategic planning for McCann-Erickson, said that the study concluded that the roaches in the pictures were all male. They were thought to symbolize the men who had abandoned these women. The sprays, Drillman explained, left the roaches squirming and "allowed the women to express their hostility toward men."

A prominent chemical company was perplexed that consumers preferred an insect spray that killed immediately over a more effective delayed-action spray that it had developed. The new spray left the insect free to crawl or fly for a while and thereby contaminate and kill others like it. A roach, for instance, might kill its entire nest of young. But a qualitative study showed that people like to see for themselves the killing power of bug spray and did not fully trust the delayed effectiveness of the new spray. This is the kind of information that simply might be missed without in-depth, face-to-face probing of consumers made possible by personal interviews and small group discussions.

Other Sources of Information

In addition to formal market and customer research, such as surveys, group discussions, and statistical analysis, some of the best sources of information about customers and competitors are a company's own employees. In firms that are obsessed with customers and leery of competitors, sales employees are integral cogs in the intelligence-gathering process. Moreover, R&D personnel and engineers are not kept isolated from customers and competitors. They accompany sales reps to talk and work with customers, they attend trade shows to meet buyers and to observe what the competition has to offer, and they keep their ears to the ground at technical seminars for possible research breakthroughs and new products by competitors. In retailing and service businesses, all the top executives, especially the CEO, need to spend perhaps one week a year working with and listening to customers in person. Few things isolate quite like the sometimes splendid accoutrements of the executive suite.

Most entrepreneurs and marketers like to rely to some extent on their intuition about which products and services will be successful and which ones will not. If they are based on experience and information, hunches can be valuable in developing and marketing products and services or in launching new businesses. But there is a distinct difference between intuition and hope, and the two are easily confused.

When an entrepreneur or executive mixes up hope with intuition, the chances of trying to build better mousetraps and making unreasonable assumptions about demand are increased dramatically. Hope is based on wishful thinking, with little or no factual information and past experience to justify it, whereas intuition is an instinct, or sharp insight, grounded in previous experience and at least some pertinent information.

Intuition and customer/market research are not substitutes for one another but are complementary. Market research can be used to test the accuracy of intuition about emerging markets and the need for new products and services. Intuition comes back into play after the research is completed, when management must choose from several courses of action.

A corporate chairman of a well-known company said that he gave up on market research because it normally told him why he should not undertake a course of action but rarely why he should. This seems to me to be an unintended recommendation for using market research. In the first place, the majority of new products do fail commercially, so negative recommendations from market research can be expected to far outnumber the positives. Secondly, if market research can identify losers with even a 70–80 percent rate of accuracy, it has been worthwhile. Executives sometimes sour on market research after they have an experience in which their studies recommend against a product that turns out to be a winner.

There is no perfect screening technique in picking winners and losers. But this is no reason to forgo customer and market research in favor of a highly intuitive, even wishful, approach to marketing and entrepreneurship. Such fly-by-the-seat-of-your-pants philosophies sooner or later lead management to trying to build better mousetraps and to practicing Chinese marketing. The entrepreneurial task is to strike a balance between conducting so much research that a paralysis-by-analysis inhibits decision making and commissioning so little research, or none at all, that management shoots from the hip.

Blunders: Oversubscribing to the Conventional Wisdom
and
Putting Too Much Faith in Forecasting

Symptoms: The entrepreneur or manager confuses strategic planning with forecasting. Planning is thought of as a by-the-numbers exercise done with computer software or on a calculator. Plans are made for a single forecasted future. Expert opinion goes largely unchallenged in formulating strategies.

Appropriate Risk Reducer: A protean company.

Like the Sea God Proteus

The motto of the World Future Society is "Tomorrow is built today." This is very true. The actions that a person (or organization) takes today go a long way to determining how he or she will fare tomorrow. Until the 1970s, getting ready for three, four, or five years hence was a matter of extrapolating current trends—it was fairly certain that the population would continue to grow at a certain rate, that Detroit would sell so many automobiles, that steelworkers' sons could count on going to work in the mills like their fathers, that gasoline prices would rise by 2 to 3 cents a year, that getting a teaching certificate would guarantee one a job, and that an executive who did an acceptable job and did not make waves could spend forty years working for General Motors, General Electric or Exxon.

Then global competition and an oil cartel changed this comforting predictability forever and, along with it, people's ability to forecast as accurately as before. Forecasters and proponents of the conventional wisdom became vulnerable to the sin of the generals—the assumption that the next war will be fought like the last war. Organizations that had assumed that the strategies that worked for them in the past would also work well in the future were chagrined to find out differently.

Individuals and companies became more accustomed to discontinuities, whether they were on Wall Street, in the Iowa farming country, in Iran, or elsewhere. The economic radar or early-warning systems that had detected impending change so consistently throughout previous years often malfunctioned. Without knowing what to expect, companies and people searched for better ways to cope with the unexpected and unpredictable.

What the more successful individuals and organizations discovered for themselves is that state-of-the-art knowledge and rapid adaptability are the keys to surviving and prospering in a sea of tumultuous change. They had to emulate the mythical Proteus, a sea god introduced by Homer in the *Odyssey,* who had the ability to change form with great alacrity. When mortals wished to consult Proteus, who enjoyed the gift of prophecy but did not want to share it with humans, he would assume any shape he desired to elude them. Only by clinging tightly to Proteus through all his changes could a mortal receive answers to his questions.

The most apt description of today's Proteus-like people and organizations was coined by Robert H. Waterman, Jr., a former consultant with McKinsey and Company but best known as the co-author of *In Search of Excellence.* Waterman says that masters of change are informed opportunists. Their main strategic advantage is information, and their primary strategic weapon is flexibility. Top executives who are informed opportunists do not set detailed strategies for their companies; they set directions and provide vision. They know that opportunity will inevitably present itself, but in subtle and unpredictable ways. Management must be able to discern emerging trends and then be committed and able to act quickly.

Informed opportunists do engage in strategic planning, but not in a highly structured way. The future is too uncertain for that. They speculate about several possible futures and develop contingency strategies for the hypothetical futures. Lee Iacocca tells of what he learned about planning from Robert McNamara, who was president of Ford Motor Company when Iacocca was a young executive there:

> "When you talked with [McNamara], you realized that he had already played out in his head the relevant details for every conceivable option and scenario. He taught me never to make a major decision without having a choice of at least vanilla or chocolate. And if more than a hundred million dollars were at stake, it was a good idea to have strawberry, too. . . . [McNamara] could carry a dozen different plans in his head. . . . Nevertheless, he taught me to put all my ideas into

writing. . . 'If you can't do that you haven't really thought it out.' " John Welch, the hard-driving change agent and taskmaster who has reshaped General Electric, wants a strategy to be summarized in a page or two. Anything longer indicates a lack of focus.

BP America's vice president for corporate planning, Heather Ross, says that the idea of strategic planning "is to anticipate what could happen and to be prepared to respond flexibly—not to forecast what will happen and get locked in." I call this process "strategic rehearsal." It is the exact reverse of the philosophy that says, "Let's wait until we get to that bridge to cross it." The knack is, first, to anticipate that we could encounter a bridge and, second, to discuss whether we would want to cross it at all. If so, let's rehearse now rather than later how we might do it. Before NASA sent astronauts to land on the moon, almost every conceivable lunar-landing situation was simulated. Just as these astronauts were prepared for a sandy, rocky, or aborted landing, so should companies be ready for several contingencies. However, in most businesses—large, medium, or small—the chief executive is tempted or lured by day-to-day pressures to fight fires instead of doing imaginative strategic thinking and working on "big picture" decisions.

Identifying plausible hypothetical futures requires entrepreneurs and companies to be keenly aware of a wide variety of areas that impinge on businesses, industries, and the economies of entire states and nations. For companies, it is here that market research and systematic environmental scanning can play vital roles. For entrepreneurs, being attuned to what is taking place in the external environment is essential—by reading, talking with people, and watching television and listening to the radio. The backgrounds of the people chosen as informal personal advisers or members of the board of directors are critical in this regard. They need to be people who see the world from the perspective of a wide-angle camera lens rather than an industry microscope. But being highly informed is only half the task. The person or company must be flexible enough to capitalize on emerging opportunities and to dodge threats. Flexibility requires companies to be able to move human and capital resources quickly to match up with opportunities. Bureaucracy and centralization of power are the enemy.

Being Innovative and Entrepreneurial

Informed opportunists are knowledge-driven people and companies with the will and ability to move fast. Companies are not lacking for advice on how they can prepare for change. However, some of the advocates speaking and writing about innovativeness and entrepreneurship make fairly sweeping generalizations concerning what managers can do to infuse creativity into their organizations. Take the idea that decentralization is the way to encourage individual initiative. In most cases this is correct; driving decisions down in the company is the best way to stay on top of customer needs and changing market conditions. But there are other situations in which centralization is better from a costs-versus-benefits standpoint. R&D often works best when it is centralized, so that a company's divisions and subsidiaries are not duplicating one another's work and can share new technology. Or a company may opt for additional centralization when it has separate sales forces calling on the same customer. One firm had sales reps from seven product lines calling regularly on the same customer.

Another caveat: If the entire organization were suddenly to become creative and entrepreneurial, anarchy would reign. What company could operate for long with entrepreneurial secretaries, accountants, computer programmers, attorneys, and human resource personnel?

One adage about running small firms says, "When two people in a business always agree, one of them is unnecessary." How true this is! Successful firms are often founded by people whose skills complement one another—a marketer and an engineer, a sales rep and an accountant, or a biologist and a general manager.

What companies, from startups to giants, need to strive for is a disciplined creativity in their quest for an innovative organization. Disciplined creativity may sound as if it is a contradiction in terms, but it is not.

The Boston Celtics professional basketball organization has consistently produced championship teams personifying creative discipline. First, there is a culture of winning, which has been established and perpetuated by Red Auerbach, initially as the coach and later as the head of basketball operations. Second, there is a disciplined system of teamwork that produces a synergy; the team is better than what you would expect if you just looked at the talents of the individual players. Third, creativity within this system comes from several star players with exceptional skills who provide leadership and are given latitude to shoot at will, while the less talented players closely follow well-defined roles expected of them by the coach.

Innovative companies are similar to the Celtics model. They employ movers and shakers, their star revenue producers, who act as change agents. Their numbers are small, but they exert great influence. And they are hard to find. As Ross Perot says about exceptional employees, "Eagles don't flock. You have to find them one at a time."

If a company is to be innovative, these movers and shakers have to be strategically placed. Certainly, either the chief executive officer or the president must be a change agent. By their actions and words, the top managers either promote or stifle creativity and risk-taking. In particular, they affect the corporate culture and control the executive incentive system.

Charles J. Pilliod, Jr. was the perceptive and innovative chairman of the Goodyear Tire & Rubber Company when the U.S. tire industry began to change over from bias-ply tires to radial tires. This was a highly significant change because of the costs of converting manufacturing facilities from bias to radial technology. Moreover, although European consumers were accustomed to radial tires—Michelin introduced the first steel-belted radial in Europe in 1948—American consumers were not. B.F. Goodrich had attempted to market radial auto tires in the United States in the early 1960s, but since the suspension systems of American cars were not designed for radials, it was unsuccessful. Goodyear was manufacturing passenger radial tires in Europe and truck radial tires in the United States in the mid-1950s but did not produce passenger radial tires for the American market until the late 1960s and early 1970s.

After Pilliod retired at Goodyear and became ambassador to Mexico, I asked him to reflect on his company's radial-tire decision in the U.S. market. His answers demonstrate the key role that a CEO must play in bringing about change in a company.

Question: When Goodyear began to convert to radial tire technology in the U.S., who made the ultimate decision to do so? How much resistance among top management in Goodyear was there to converting to radial passenger tire technology? What were the major objections?

Pilliod: The decision to convert Goodyear to radial tires was mine, and while there was some resistance from members of management, it was based primarily on the reluctance of major original equipment manufacturers [U.S. automobile producers] who had not at that time shown a readiness to accept radials. They were concerned both with the quality and their feeling that the public would not be prepared to pay the higher price.

Question: Why is there often so much resistance to change in companies, and what can top management do to promote change?

Pilliod: There's a very human tendency among individuals, particularly in a large organization, to find comfort and a feeling of security in situations and associations to which they have become accustomed over a number of years. When they are asked to change their thinking—for example, to "anticipate" in the early 1970s that tire markets would begin swinging toward radial construction—many are prone to resist, at least passively. It is difficult to give up tried and true situations of the past for the unknowns of the future. In such situations, it is up to top management to make it uncomfortable to cling to the past; to make looking to the future and acting accordingly a condition of comfort, security, and rewards.

Question: How much do you feel that your international experience helped you in your role of CEO?

Pilliod: Time has shown that the United States is just one more country in the world market. We have no particular advantages or disadvantages. But the greater the knowledge we have of our competition, which is often of another nationality, the more opportunity we have to compete successfully. I feel my knowledge of world marketing and my international experience stood me in good stead in my role as CEO of Goodyear.

Besides the chief executive officer, movers and shakers must be well represented in marketing, R&D, and manufacturing if the company is to develop and make the new and quality products it will need to compete effectively. Strategic planning, too often a bastion of bureaucracy and number-crunching, needs to be aggressive in searching for emerging and hypothetical opportunities and threats. Like the Celtics, the innovative company will need solid role players—professionals, administrators, and functionaries—who are good at what they do, to support and assist in implementing the company's revenue-producing efforts.

Geneticists have a concept they call "hybrid vigor." This refers to the invigorating effect that introducing a new gene pool into a closely bred line can have on the offspring. That is why a puppy of mixed heritage—a "Heinz 57 dog"—often turns out to be hardier and smarter than a registered purebred, especially if the purebred is inbred. Companies can achieve this hybrid vigor effect, too, by introducing new blood into the organization. Companies that have a policy of promoting only from within eventually stagnate. A culture of "our way of doing things" takes over, and the adage "if it ain't broke, don't fix it" becomes ingrained. New blood might say instead, "If it ain't broke, at least look at the possibility of changing it for the better." This is the kind of never-satisfied attitude that fosters innovation and keeps the company's competitive edge sharp.

In a small company, the president is normally the change agent and must rely heavily on his or her own instincts. A small firm does not have the luxury of hiring a cadre of movers and shakers, which is why people with dissimilar but complementary talents often make successful partners in new business ventures. Not only does the small firm get the benefit of different kinds of expertise, it also usually obtains a variety of perspectives—a dose of organizational hybrid vigor.

The stereotype of the innovative business person, the mover and shaker entrepreneur, is the Donald Trump or Ted Turner type, a consummate real estate deal-maker or a flamboyant captain-outrageous media mogul hell-bent to build an empire. But the stereotype is wrong. Entrepreneurs are generally more cerebral in their approach and are not colorful characters. A psychological survey by *Inc.* magazine of 151 chief executives of the fastest-growing small firms in the United States found that these entrepreneurs are mostly quiet, introspective people who focus on ideas, logic, and perceptions, a description resembling the classic profile of a college professor.

Blunders: Selling Too Much Sizzle, Not Enough Steak
and
Confusing Financial/Marketing Cause and Effect

Symptoms: Through words and deeds, management makes it clear that short-term profitability is what it is after. It is "bottom-line" this and "bottom-line" that to the detriment of investing in the things that will enable the company to be an informed opportunist and a profitable long-term competitor—customer research, developing new products and services, improving quality, and augmenting marketing capability and company image.

Appropriate Risk Reducers:

• A unifying, unambiguous, written, and well-publicized business definition that identifies senior management's strategic vision for the company. Northrop Corporation has captured the essential ingredients with a statement in its annual report: "Northrop is a defense company supplying the United States and foreign allies with timely and cost efficient state of the art military aircrafts, electronics systems, and support services." Can there be any doubt about what customers, what needs, what products, and what markets Northrop intends to pursue, or about its commitment to leading-edge technology and efficiency?

• A corporate environment or culture built squarely on two eternal verities: that superior product/service value to customers and devotion to long-term market development are the only ways to build and sustain a company's competitive position. Senior management, by their words and actions but mostly by their actions, determines the extent to which this kind of culture prevails. Unfortunately, when all is said and done, more is usually said than done. Words from top management that are not acted upon soon take on a hollow ring.

Doing the Right Things and Doing Things Right

Is it more important to do the right things or to do things right? This question probes the importance of strategic effectiveness versus operational efficiency. If one were forced to choose between the two, doing the right things is more important than doing things right. No matter how efficient you became at making iceboxes, you would not sell many in head-to-head competition with refrigerators. No matter how efficiently you operate a warehouse in Montana, it will be of no value if the warehouse is needed in New Jersey. The "right things" to do would be to not manufacture iceboxes at all and to locate the warehouse in the East.

In today's highly competitive world environment, however, it is no longer a choice between doing the right things and doing things right. At one time, when there was not much foreign competition, a U.S. company might sell a lot of, say, TVs, even if they were not of the highest quality. This is no longer possible. If a company is to be successful over the long haul, it must perform effectively in strategy and efficiently in operations. It is not enough for senior management to identify which letters of the alphabet spell out the right market strategy. Competition requires top management to make sure that the i's get dotted and the t's get crossed with tactical precision. Managers reap what they sow. If they choose the right industries and deliver quality products and services, their companies will grow and prosper. On the other hand, if, in the interests of the short-term bottom line, they choose to minimize spending for R&D, automation, marketing, worker training, or other contributors to long-term market development, then their companies will grow uncompetitive.

The hackneyed phrase "bottom line" is philosophically antithetical to building a company into a winner. It diverts attention from the long term to the short term. Drive through Gary, Indiana, and take a look at the depressing steel mills using outmoded technology because steel industry executives of yesteryear were myopically bottom-line-oriented. As of the late 1980s, U.S. firms in electronics manufacturing reject 8 to 10 percent of their own output because of quality defects, compared with only 1 percent or less for the Japanese. The average age of manufacturing equipment in the U.S. for all industries is seventeen years, as opposed to ten years in Japan. In average annual spending growth for factory automation, the United States trails behind Europe, Japan, and Asia. The Japanese have increased their annual investment per worker by 90 percent since 1975, compared to 25 percent in the United States. From the time U.S. manufacturers receive an order to the time they ship it, on average, 5 to 6 months goes by; in Japan it takes 1 to 2 months. How about average annual growth in manufacturing productivity between 1979 and 1986? The United States finished fifth—behind Japan, Britain, France, and Italy.

Toyota spent hours individually screening and interviewing prospective production workers for its plant in Georgetown, Kentucky, to determine if each applicant had the right work ethic. Contrast this with the traditional show-up-at-the-plant-gate approach in American companies. No amount of marketing acumen and skill, no amount of sizzle, can offset quality, cost, and delivery-time disadvantages for long—and it is a monumental blunder to attempt it. Buyers remember unfulfilled promises. And competitors are quick to remind them in case they do forget.

Malcolm Forbes has warned of what American companies must do if they are to compete effectively in global competition:

> Our companies, both great and planning to be, had better right soon start picking CEOs who know how to make things, make services work; who know how to *sell.* We have had enough—more than enough—of balance-sheet whizzes, of ledger leger-demain; enough of accountants' unimaginative sharp-pencil wanding; enough of sweeping, swooping, preying legal eagles. With CEOs who know how to *manufacture,* to *motivate,* to *innovate,* and to *sell* back at the helm, there are no ceilings on the heights our businesses can scale in the vast marketplaces of the Free World.

On the Track to Nowhere or Somewhere?

Kenny Rogers, in the classic song "The Gambler," weaves a tale of his haunting meeting with an old and savvy gambler on a warm summer evening on a train bound for nowhere. In return for a drink of whiskey and a smoke, the crafty gambler, just before he dies in his seat, gives Rogers, who looks as though he is out of aces, advice about living gleaned from years of playing cards. The best-known of the gambler's counsel is the lyric that in order to survive "you got to know when to hold them, when to fold them."

The dying gambler's folk wisdom has plenty to offer to people starting and managing businesses. When it comes to new products, services, and ventures, there are basically two ways to go—on the track bound for somewhere or the more traveled route to nowhere. Knowing when one's on the right track, and thus when to hold or fold, is rarely clear; if it were, the failure rate for new products, services, and businesses would not be so high. Informed opportunists do a better job of knowing than most.

The six timeless marketing blunders are responsible for countless business failures, often needlessly so. By being ever-aware of the pitfalls of the six, remaining objective, and taking precautionary steps, the entrepreneur or marketer has a fighting chance to succeed. He or she may still be derailed by poor implementation and management, lack of capital, or external circumstances beyond control. But, conceptually, the cornerstone for building a business, commercializing a product, or introducing a service is in place. The business is on the track to somewhere.

Notes

Chapter 1

Page
1   David L. Birch, "Down, But Not Out," *Inc.,* May 1988, pp. 20–21.
1–2 Jonathan Clements, "The Turbulent Job Market," *Forbes,* July 13, 1987, pp. 114–19.
2   David E. Gumpert, "Each Year, a Million New Businesses," *The New York Times,* April 17, 1988, p. F-17.
2   "Change, Schumpeter said": For an excellent summary of Schumpeter's ideas about economic change, see William Baldwin, "Creative Destruction," *Forbes,* July 13, 1987.
3   "Only a very few families": Edward F. Cone, "Preserving the Family Fortune," *Forbes,* June 27, 1988, p. 185.
3   "a Daniel Boone–type pioneer": Marc Beauchamp, "Under the Gun," *Forbes,* June 13, 1988.

Chapter 2

8–9   "Public utilities test": Marc Beauchamp, "Cold Shoulder," *Forbes,* October 6, 1986, p. 168.
11   "a technological success": "The Anatomy of RCA's Videodisc Failure," *Business Week,* April 23, 1984, p. 89.
10–12 For an excellent chronology of events concerning RCA's SelectaVision and the videodisc industry, see Kenneth L. Bernhardt and Thomas C. Kinnear, *Cases in Marketing Management* (Plano, Texas: Business Publications, 1988), pp. 46–59.

Chapter 3

25   "It's a lot easier": James Koch, "Portrait of the CEO as Salesman." Reprinted with permission, *Inc.,* March 1988. Copyright © 1988 by *Inc.* Publishing Company, 38 Commercial Wharf, Boston, MA 02110.

Page
  26   "I began by telling": Ibid.
  27   "Abraham Lincoln": Thomas Keiser, " 'The Illinois Beast': One of Our
       Greatest Presidents," *The Wall Street Journal,* February 11, 1988, p. 22.
31–32   "a brand-new car": Copyright © 1985 by Rinfret Associates, Inc. All
       rights reserved. Reprinted with permission.
  34   "A dinner he had with Andre Heiniger": Mark H. McCormack, *What
       They Don't Teach You at Harvard Business School* (New York: Ban-
       tam Books, 1984), pp. 53, 113.
  38   "Ford counters": Jacob M. Schlesinger, "Ford's Claims About Quali-
       ty Show Difficulty of Identifying Top Autos," *The Wall Street Jour-
       nal,* March 14, 1988, p. 21.
  39   "Ford says it has": Ibid.
  39   "Ogilvy observes that": "A Disease Called Entertainment," *Forbes,*
       March 7, 1988, pp. 150–51.
  43   "PIMS has found": Robert D. Buzzell and Bradley T. Gale, *The PIMS
       Principles* (New York: The Free Press, 1987), pp. 107–109.
  44   "American companies are responding": Christopher Knowlton, "What
       America Makes Best," *Fortune,* March 28, 1988, pp. 40–54.
  45   "BMW of North America": "Be Nice to Customers; They Set Your Pay,
       Some Companies Tell Managers," *The Wall Street Journal,* March 3,
       1988, p. 1.

Chapter 4

  49   "Progress does not follow": An Wang, *Lessons* (Reading, MA:
       Addison-Wesley, 1986), p. 2.
  49   "Conceal or ignore": Ibid.
  50   "the world's food supply": Thomas Sowell, "The Overpopulations
       Have it Exactly Wrong," *The (Cleveland) Plain Dealer,* May 14,
       1988, p. 18B.
  51   "For years, physicians subscribed": Larry Thompson, "New Theory
       Explains Tremors After Surgery," *Washington Post* (Health), March
       1, 1988, p. 5.
54–55   "the prevailing wisdom in Japan": Simon Ramo, "How to Revive U.S.
       High Tech," *Fortune,* May 9, 1988, p. 126.
  55   "In the late 1980s": "A Muddled Market: Seniors' Numbers," *The Wall
       Street Journal,* October 12, 1987, p. 21.
55–56   "different consumption patterns": Ibid.
  56   "the Hispanic population": Jose De Cordoba, "More Firms Court
       Hispanic Consumers—But Find Them a Tough Market to Target,"
       The Wall Street Journal, February 25, 1988, p. 25.
  57   "a study by Find/SVP": "Who are the Rich?" *Forbes,* April 20, 1987,
       p. 12.
  57   "Income concentration in the United States": "Das Kapital (Revised
       Edition)," *The Wall Street Journal,* October 7, 1986, p. 32.

Page
58 "The very same month": Susan Lee and Tatiana Pouschine, "Are We a Nation of Spendthrifts?" *Forbes,* December 16, 1985, pp. 128–34.

58–59 "statistic after statistic": Ben J. Wattenberg, *The Good News is the Bad News is Wrong* (New York: Simon & Schuster, 1985).

59–60 "Vacuum tubes are gone": Mimi Bluestone, "Can Vacuum-Tube Valley Be Far Behind?" *Business Week,* June 27, 1988, p. 92.

62 "One mistake in global marketing": Stephen Karel, "Details, Details," *Consumer Markets Abroad,* May 1988, p. 1.

Chapter 5

71 "forecasts from its 1971 article": Dean S. Ammer, "What Businessmen Expect From the 1970s," *Harvard Business Review,* January-February 1971, p. 41.

77–78 "A Sampling of *Omni* Forecasts": "*Omni* Forecasts." *The World Almanac & Book of Facts,* 1986 edition, copyright © Newspaper Enterprise Association, Inc. 1985, New York, NY 10166. Reprinted with permission.

78 "A Sampling of World Future Society Forecasts": Reprinted by permission of the World Future Society, 4916 Saint Elmo Avenue, Bethesda, Maryland 20814.

82 "Gallium Gulch, California": Kathleen K. Wiegner, "Silicon Valley 1, Gallium Gulch 0," *Forbes,* January 11, 1988, pp. 270–72.

84 "An associate and I researched": Susan Higgins and William L. Shanklin, "A Study of High-Tech Consumer Product Buyer Behavior," in William L. Shanklin and John K. Ryans, Jr., *Essentials of Marketing High Technology* (Lexington, MA: Lexington Books, 1987), pp. 183–84.

86 "the Seer-Sucker Theory": J. Scott Armstrong, "How Expert Are the Experts?" *Inc.,* December 1981, pp. 15–16.

Chapter 6

90 "When working out figures": Carl Crow, *Four Hundred Million Customers* (New York: Halycon House, 1937), pp. 302–304.

90–91 "But, while a few": Ibid., p. 309.

92 "Kay Fishburn, a nurse": Rose Gutfeld, "Why Not Simply Ask 147 People To Give a Billion Dollars Each?," *The Wall Street Journal,* March 21, 1988, p. 17.

92 "An organization calling itself": "100 Billionaires Invited to Create a Disease-free, Problem-free Peaceful World Family—Heaven on Earth," advertisement in *The Wall Street Journal,* April 14, 1988, p. 2.

93 "Study after study": For an in-depth look at actual data on the association between market share and profitability, the reader may want to consult Robert D. Buzzell and Bradley T. Gale, *The PIMS Principles* (New York: The Free Press, 1987), pp. 70–102.

Page
94 "Over a twenty-five-year period": Laurie Hays, "Du Pont's Difficulties In Selling Kevlar Show Hurdles of Innovation," *The Wall Street Journal*, September 29, 1987, pp. 1, 23.

Chapter 7

107 "Most people are surprised": Panhandle Eastern Corporation, "John Wooden on Staying Power," public relations release, Houston, Texas. Reprinted by permission.

109 "Companies like Kohlberg Kravis Roberts": See Carol J. Loomis, "Buyout Kings," *Fortune*, July 4, 1988, pp. 53–60.

109 "Describing his strategy": Peter Petre, "The Greatest Capitalist in History," *Fortune*, August 31, 1987, p. 34.

109–110 "what occurred at TWA": Linda Sandler, "Icahn's Bid for Texaco Questioned by Analysts Who Criticize His Capital Spending for TWA," *The Wall Street Journal*, June 15, 1988, p. 53.

111 "Rubbermaid's objective": "Profiles in Leadership," *World*, Fall 1987, p. 35.

111 "Similarly, more than 25 percent": Kenneth Labich, "The Innovators," *Fortune*, June 6, 1988, p. 50.

111 "Rubbermaid's chairman": "Profiles in Leadership," p. 35.

111–112 "James Burke is now": H. John Steinbreder, "Taking Chances at J&J," *Fortune*, June 6, 1988, p. 60.

112 "SmithKline Beckman, a pharmaceutical company": Labich, "The Innovators," p. 53.

114–115 "The Strategic Planning Institute": Robert D. Buzzell and Bradley T. Gale, *The PIMS Principles* (New York: The Free Press, 1987), pp. 217, 226.

115 "The companies that spend heavily on research": William L. Shanklin and John K. Ryans, Jr., "Organizing for High-Tech Marketing," *Harvard Business Review*, November–December 1984, pp. 164–71; Peter F. Drucker, "Best R&D is Business-Driven," *The Wall Street Journal*, February 10, 1988, p. 18.

116 "Rubbermaid, although it did not": Regina Brett, "Rubbermaid's Fingers on Consumers' Pulse," (Akron) *Beacon Journal*, March 14, 1988, p. B-1.

117 "Lee A. Iacocca, describing": Lee Iacocca with William Novak, *Iacocca* (New York: Bantam Books, 1985), p. 44.

119 "Walter R. Lovejoy": "Planning Without Calculators," *Inc.*, November 1985, p. 130.

119–120 "Robert J. Crowley": Erik Larson, "The Best-Laid Plans," *Inc.*, February 1987, p. 64.

120 "As another venture capitalist": Quotes are from Margaret L.H. Ross, *An Exploration into the Role of Marketing in the Venture*

Page

        Capital Investment Evaluation Process for High-Technology Startup Companies, unpublished doctoral dissertation, Kent State University, 1987. Reprinted by permission.

121–122 "Revlon is a good example": Anthony Ramirez, "The Raider Who Runs Revlon," *Fortune,* September 14, 1987, pp. 56–63.

122 "Take Allegis, formerly United Airlines": Stratford P. Sherman, "The Trio That Humbled Allegis," *Fortune,* July 20, 1987, pp. 52–59.

122 "the wave of corporate restructurings": William D. Marbach with Emily T. Smith, "A Perilous Cutback in Research Spending," *Business Week,* June 20, 1988, p. 139.

124 "In Japan, stockholders": James F. Schrager and Julian Gresser, "Going Public, Japanese Style," *The Wall Street Journal,* May 2, 1988, p. 18.

124–125 "Malcolm S. Forbes, editor-in-chief": Malcolm S. Forbes, "Fact and Comment," *Forbes,* June 27, 1988, p. 32. Reprinted with permission.

125 Sherry Siegel, "Selling Your Way to the Top," *Success,* January–February 1987, pp. 40–46.

Chapter 8

130–131 "The McCann-Erickson advertising agency": Ronald Alsop, "Advertisers Put Consumers on the Couch," *The Wall Street Journal,* May 13, 1988, p. 17.

134 "They had to emulate the mythical Proteus": For an excellent article about Proteus-type companies, see Susan Lee and Christie Brown, "The Protean Corporation," *Forbes,* August 24, 1987, pp. 76–79.

134 "The most apt description": Robert H. Waterman, Jr., *The Renewal Factor* (New York: Bantam Books, 1987), p. 6.

134–135 "Lee Iacocca tells": Lee Iacocca with William Novak, *Iacocca* (New York: Bantam Books, 1984), pp. 42–43.

135 "BP America's vice president": Jim Marino, "Preparing for Uncertainty," *Scene,* Winter 1988, p. 10.

139 "A psychological survey," "The Entrepreneurial Personality," *Inc.,* August 1988, p. 18.

141–142 "As of the late 1980s": Karen Pennar, "The Productivity Paradox," *Business Week,* June 6, 1988, p. 102.

142 Malcolm S. Forbes, "Put Those Who Can Make and/or Sell Back at the Helm," *Forbes,* August 8, 1988, p. 17. Reprinted with permission.

Index

About the Author

W illiam L. Shanklin is a consultant, educator, speaker, and prize-winning author. His associations have ranged from major companies to startup ventures. He holds a doctorate in business administration from the University of Maryland and currently specializes in marketing strategy and entrepreneurship at the Kent State University Graduate School of Management in Ohio.